PARENTING
Beyond Your
UPBRINGING

Denise Copp Engelbrecht

Oxford Advanced Learner's Dictionary of Current English / [by] A.S. Hornby; Editor Jonathan Crowther. Oxford, England :Oxford University Press, 1995.

Contents

FORWARD

The moment your child took his or her first breath you may have felt as unequipped as I did. I remember that day when our daughter was born, almost 40 years ago. As I looked at her precious fingers and toes, I was more aware than ever of how fragile she was and how unequipped I was. Children are a precious gift from God. You love them deeply, but you find yourself scrambling for the instruction book on how to care for them. Like myself, most parents enter into parenting with only the family model of how they were raised.

Parenting is not a casual hobby that you can try out to see if you like and then lay it down. Parenting is a lifetime commitment as you seek to nurture, train and provide the best environment possible so your children can thrive. The joy of parenting is far greater than you can ever imagine as you watch your child grow and develop.

Healing from your own painful childhood experiences will assure that your parenting can be successful. Parenting must be an intentional pursuit as you seek God to heal from your own parents' mistakes in order to break the dysfunctional cycles that the pain created.

When I met Denise, she had worked through a lot of personal healing from her own childhood wounds. She had even published her first book on the subject. We had much in common; first of all, our love for God and a passion for our family. The second thing we had in common was our name; "Denise," which has a Christian meaning of one who is "dedicated to God." We discovered we were both dedicated to God, and from an incredibly young age felt called by God to heal from our own painful childhood experiences. We share the same passion to see others healed from the pain of their upbringings so they do not pass the same pain on to the next generation.

Shortly after Denise attended a "Healing the Heart" retreat she approached my husband and me with the desire to take the Advanced Training that we offered and merge the healing principles she learned from our ministry into her parenting book. We gladly agreed and are excited and honored to endorse her book.

In this new revised version of her book, Parenting Beyond Your Upbringing, she explains that the only way to break the cycles of pain and dysfunction is through the healing of your own heart. When we parent out of our own pain, we will soon see our children struggling with the same issues of depression, angry responses and even addictions we have fought to overcome.

Denise provides a wealth of knowledge that she has gained from her own experiences of parenting her seven children from a healed position. From her own story, growing up in a dysfunctional home and seeing the devastating effect it had on herself and her siblings she began the quest to find healing so she would not make the same mistakes. I love what Denise says: "As parents, our experiences of yesterday can affect our fruit in parenting today." This is so true and Denise knew that to parent her children beyond her own upbringing she had to find a safe place for healing.

This book will bring healing and empowerment as you parent your children beyond your own painful upbringing. I believe that if you apply the principles you will learn in this book you will see amazing results in the lives of your children.

God bless you!

Denise Boggs
Living Waters Ministry
www.livingwaersminisry.com

As you read this book you may want personal guidance and help along the way.

We want to walk with you on this parenting journey. We have resources available that will help you connect emotionally to your children so that you can lead them effectively with love, confidence, and grace.

Please visit us at
BeyondYourUpbringing.com
to learn more.

INTRODUCTION

Have you ever found yourself wondering why you feel stuck in defective parenting cycles? Statistics show that people raised in less than perfect homes (all of us) will most likely repeat the patterns of dysfunction, causing the issues to be passed to yet another generation. Unfortunately, some cycles are more broken than others.

We don't have to repeat the same dysfunctional patterns of our upbringing. Whether you were raised in an abusive household or an imperfect one, you can rise above the challenges and break the cycles. We can bridge the gap and disrupt the pitfalls in our families. We can create the change to make our next generation stronger and better.

I dealt with a lot of physical, emotional trauma, and dysfunction in my household growing up. I knew that I didn't want the same for my family. My siblings found their "fixes" in life, numbing their pain with drugs and alcohol. I knew, for me, that wasn't the answer and that I had to find a "fix" that would carry me through life and give me stability. I saw how my siblings' lifestyles of numbing their pain destroyed their lives and increased the severity of the dysfunction. I knew that God held my answers in His hands, and if I could hold onto Him and not let go, I would escape the devastating cycle of dysfunction for myself and my children. As I clung to God, I had to do my part. My heart needed to heal from the pain of my past to become the parent I wanted to be. Even though I wanted something different for my family, I unknowingly parented from a deficit of love stemming from my upbringing. Therefore, I had nothing of substance to give to my children. I had to learn how to let God heal my brokenness so that I could be filled with His love and then reciprocate it to my children.

You may be thinking to yourself, "I had a pretty good childhood." This may be the case, but I've found nobody has perfect parents. Therefore we can use our parents' ceiling as our step stool as we benefit from an in-depth look at how we can rise above the shortfalls of our upbringing. The end goal for our household should be to create a safe and secure home for our children to grow and blossom into the healthy people God created them to be. A safe household is where children are protected, nurtured, accepted and unconditionally loved. A safe home is also where everyone feels secure to talk about their thoughts and feelings.

Our experiences of yesterday can affect our fruit in parenting today. Therefore, to establish a safe home for our children, we need to evaluate our parenting behaviors today and recognize if our past is tainting them. As we pinpoint undesirable fruit, we can then take action to deal with the root of the problems to create better parenting responses.

As I was determined to break the defective patterns in parenting, I followed a plan or the following steps to gain P.O.W.E.R. over my brokenness:

- Pinpoint the problem
- Overcome victimhood
- Walk in forgiveness
- Embrace new thinking
- Release people and Resist old patterns

As I've taken these principles and applied them to my life, I've been able to, along with my husband, break the dysfunctional patterns in our family. We don't have to be stuck in the rut of unsuccessful parental behaviors. We can have an amazing life and a remarkably happy family. I was determined to create the close-knit, happy, healthy family; one that I didn't have growing up. With determination, you can do it too.

As our children become adults, it's incredible to see them being successful. Our children will pass along more stable and functional parenting to our future generations.

As parents, we are leaving a legacy, teaching our children by example. But, we can choose whether we leave a good, strong legacy or not.
I believe that if you apply the life lessons I share in this book you'll be able to break free from whatever is holding you back, just like I did.

SECTION 1

GOING BACK TO
MOVE FORWARD

CHAPTER 1

THE GOOD, THE BAD, THE UGLY

A s I share a glimpse of my story, you may see parts of your story in mine. Take note of your thoughts and feelings as you read. Sometimes we must reach back into our yesterday to deal with the fruit of today. As we go from chapter to chapter, you and I will put the pieces together and I will give you the tools you need to become the stronger, more successful parent you want to be.

Daddy's Little Girl

When I was a little girl, my daddy was my hero-my prince. I was "the apple of his eye." He could do no wrong. But at four years old, just as I thought everything was perfect in my little world, life came crashing down. I woke up one morning and my daddy was gone. My world revolved around my daddy, so what was I to do now? What little girl's life does not revolve around her daddy? I just couldn't understand why he would leave us. I thought that he loved me and that I was special to him. I felt lonely and abandoned. Did I do something wrong? Was I not good enough to keep him from leaving me? Maybe he didn't love me anymore? Was I unlovable? All of these lies flooded my little brain. Those questions haunted me and kept me stuck for many years to come. To make matters worse, my brother and I were not able to see my father after he left. I yearned to see my dad and connect with him. My mother wouldn't allow us to communicate with him at all. Also, we were forbidden to see any part of my father's side of the family. I felt a big hole in my heart. This was very traumatic and painful as I was very close with my father's side of the family, especially my great-grandparents. They were the only source of nurturing, love, and affection that I desperately needed. They made me feel special. I felt peaceful, safe, and unconditionally loved when I was with them.

As God created the family, He made us to feel complete as both the mother and father are present to take care of us. Subconsciously, in the depths of our soul, we recognize when one or more of the components of the family unit is missing. When my father and grandparents were taken from my life, it created a longing and aching inside of me to be reconnected with them. Did you have both parents present, emotionally and physically?

The bond I had with my great-grandparents was exceptionally strong. I remember every morning my great-grandmother would bring me a little glass of milk and orange juice in bed. This made me feel like a princess. She sat and talked to me about things that I thought were important and listened to me. She gave me the attention that I didn't receive at home. I remembered quality time spent over special shopping outings, reading books, cuddling and all the bonding a four-year-old needs. My great-grandmother talked to me about God and prayed with me every night before I went to sleep, and they often took me to church on Sunday. They were the only Christian influences I had in my life at that time.

After my dad left, we had several potential father figures pass through our lives, sometimes weekly. Looking and yearning for a father figure, I always wondered which one would be my "new dad." The men that my mother brought around were very abusive, verbally, physically, and sexually. You see, my mother grew up in an abusive home. That's what she knew.

Repeating the pattern of her childhood, she was attracted to abusive men. So often, we see generational patterns repeating over and over. We become familiar or comfortable or feel like this is just what life is supposed to be (because it's all we've ever known), so we carry it out in our next generation. When I was nine, my mom met a man that became my predominant father figure and I considered him my step-father. He brought a sense of stability to our family for a little while. For the first year he was with us, we were happy. I felt like we had a normal family. Then, everything changed. He started drinking excessively and became belligerent and mean. He became one of the main contributors to physical, verbal, and emotional abuse.

The abuse we went through was pretty severe. I remember moments when I thought my siblings weren't going to make it out alive. I was the peacemaker of the family, so I would always stand back, yelling at the abuser who was beating my brothers or sister. Telling them, "STOP, STOP, STOP." All my yelling did not stop the beatings. It made me feel helpless, insecure and always scared.

Here's one story to give you a glimpse of what I'm talking about. I was five and my baby brother was three. My brother was just a normal, curious toddler investigating his surroundings. He picked up a lighter that was sitting on the stand. As my brother toddled around holding the lighter, the man that was taking care of us at the time decided to teach my brother a lesson (not to play with lighters). He picked my brother up and pried the lighter from his pudgy hands and started to burn his fingers over and over again. My baby brother was screaming in pain and fear, but the adult wouldn't stop. I kept yelling for the person to STOP, but he didn't listen. By the time he was done burning my brother with the lighter, he had severe burns all over his hands. The skin was severely blistered. I felt so helpless and hopeless. I did not feel like we were ever safe or secure from harm at any given moment.

The Point that Changed Everything for Me

My mom started sending us to church on the church bus. I think she just wanted to get rid of us a little while to have some quiet time on Sundays. In church, I found hope that not everyone was bad and mean and that happy families existed. Even at a young age, I knew that I wanted something different when I grew up. I wanted a happy family just like I saw at church. Church was one of the only places that I felt safe, secure and stable. A year later, when I was nine, I went to a day camp with Pioneer Girls, a Christian group. I dedicated my life to Jesus that day. I remember vividly feeling so different, physically and emotionally. Physically, I felt like my body was so light that I could almost fly away. Emotionally, I felt incredibly happy, whole, and complete.

Reunion and Disappointment

I was reintroduced to my biological father when I was about thirteen. The reality of being reunited with him didn't match my hopes and dreams. I realized quickly that my dad was not the "knight in shining armor" that I had remembered as a little girl. He didn't seem to know how to love me the way I needed him to. He stayed in his own world, watching tv and was very disconnected. He was "there" physically but not emotionally. I had always imagined that when we met again, we would sit and talk and really get to know each other, but we didn't. I left that weekend feeling emptier and lonelier than I did before. My dreams of having a relationship with him seemed even more unattainable.

My feelings of disappointment and loss that weekend were compounded as I felt like my position as "Daddy's little girl" had been taken by my younger half-sister. In dealing with my father's aloofness, it certainly seemed that way. During this weekend reunion, my half-sister and I got into a terrible argument over needing to share our father with each other. This was such a gut-wrenching experience because, for nearly a decade, I had dreamt of once again being daddy's little girl. Now she had taken my place.

Later, I learned he simply didn't know how to be a dad to me. Eventually, I had to come to terms with the fact that he wasn't going to be able to give me the father/daughter relationship I yearned for. He was pouring from an empty cup. As I began to understand he couldn't give me what he didn't have, it gave me a level of grace to release a portion of the rejection I had carried all of those years.

Sometimes just understanding the cause behind our parents' shortcomings helps us gain a new perspective in dealing with the pain from childhood, and as a result, helps us respond differently as parents going forward.

I Saw the Difference

I had two older siblings and a younger brother. My older brother was nine years older than me, and my sister was eight years older. My older siblings and eventually younger brother chose to deal with the pain of our dysfunctional family by abusing drugs and alcohol. My brothers were regularly in trouble, in and out of jail for drug and alcohol abuse. My sister also found her comfort in self-medicating with substances. I realized I needed to respond to the pain differently than my siblings. Even though we all grew up in the same house with the same upbringing, when times got tough I ran TO God and they ran AWAY from God. My siblings found temporary comfort in chemical substances, and I found comfort in my faith. I watched how my siblings gained temporary happiness with long-term damage to themselves as well as those around them. I didn't want temporary happiness. I wanted a solution to help me and my future. I found that my faith gave me that comfort and stability I needed to sustain me through the good and bad times. It's what gave me the ability to rise above my circumstances and gain victory in the end.

As my siblings fell deeper and deeper into drug use, I felt abandoned by them. My sister was like a second mother to me before I lost her to her devices. Our relationships grew further, and further apart; it felt like we were strangers. It seemed like they entered into an utterly different world from mine. Again, I felt all alone.

Not Fitting In

At school, I was socially awkward and seemed to be different from the other kids. I was bullied a great deal, and I just couldn't figure out how to fit in. I felt like I had a label on my forehead or something. Could it be that I was just unloveable? Unlikeable? Was there something wrong with me?

At 13, I started competing in pageants. Being on stage provided me with the attention I never got from my parents or others. For once, I didn't feel invisible. I learned how to apply makeup, dress up, look and speak confidently, along with being pretty. This lifestyle set me up for a lifetime of performing. If I looked good and could be good enough, then I could gain the attention of my mother and other people. I gained a false sense of value from performing and "looking the part." For a moment while on stage, I felt valuable. It felt good. For brief moments, it gave me the courage and the confidence to face the turmoil that was going on in my home.

What makes you feel valued? Do you have to earn it or do you have a sense of confidence in who you are?

Even though the pageants helped me in some areas of life, as I started high school, they became one more thing for kids to tease me about. The kids could see past the false sense of confidence that I had gained.

I was told, "Be yourself, and people will like you." I didn't know who I was, let alone how to be myself. I was so afraid of rejection that I would become whoever people wanted me to be. I wore many masks so people would like me. The problem with that was people could see the "masks" and I was constantly misunderstood. I didn't know how to be real. This perpetuated the cycle of rejection.

My high school years quickly became the most challenging time in my life. At this time, the physical, verbal, and emotional abuse at school collided with the ever-increasing abuse at home. I felt suicidal and numb. People naively told me to smile, but that's the last thing I felt like doing. I hated life, and I just wanted to curl up in a ball and disappear. I couldn't deal with it anymore. I didn't feel accepted by my peers, and I didn't feel loved at home. I didn't want to live. My grades went from High Honor Roll (A's) to failing. I felt like no matter how hard I tried, I couldn't win. The teachings from church were no longer able to help me bear the pain. I was tired of fighting against the current. The non-stop abuse was wearing me down fast. I felt like I was drowning. It was at this point that I lost all ability to feel emotion. No matter what was happening around me, I didn't have "feelings" about anything.

Losing My Brother

In my junior year of high school, we got an urgent phone call. We learned that my oldest brother had been in a terrible accident. He was living in Florida at the time, and we lived in New York. The doctors called and told us to come to the hospital immediately as he was in critical condition.

We found out that he had been in the bar all night drinking and had been consuming drugs all day. He came out of the bar, drunk and high. While crossing the street, he got hit by a car. The car threw him up in the air and across the road. Due to the severity of his injuries, they airlifted him to the nearest hospital. He had massive brain injuries and went into a coma. Doctors removed a significant portion of his brain because of damage and to control the bleeding.

When I was finally able to see my brother, he was still in a coma. Seeing him like this was disturbing. He didn't look like himself at all. His face was distorted and sunken in from the surgery that removed part of his skull and brain. He was attached to all sorts of machines, tubes and wires. He couldn't talk to me, but I knew that he could hear everything I said to him. I could tell that he was actually trying to respond to me. I told him that I loved him and that I was praying for him. After four months in a coma, he passed away.

I remember the whole time I visited him in the hospital and at his funeral, I felt numb. I was not able to feel my emotions like I should have. I wasn't able to process my pain and loss and was not even able to cry. It was frustrating to know that the loss of my brother was devastating, but I couldn't respond with proper emotions that could help me grieve. I was shut down and couldn't feel a thing.

Beyond the numbness, I felt a great deal of guilt. When my brother was up in New York a few months prior, I tried to help him get off drugs and help him gain some sense of stability in life with a job. My brother and I had a strong bond, and I wanted to keep him from moving back to Florida. After a couple of weeks trying to be "his savior," my brother couldn't rise above the darkness that kept him bound. He moved back to Florida and continued the devastating cycle of destruction. I felt like a failure. I kept thinking if only I had tried harder, I might have been able to help him. This belief was a lie that tormented me for years after his death.

At this point in my life, I had gone through so much pain. I learned to cope with it by stuffing my feelings. I couldn't talk about the pain, so I ignored it when it surfaced and pretended like it wasn't there. This way of coping worked for a short time until everything built up and I became more and more filled with unresolved pain and bitterness. It became a way of life, ignoring my feelings. When life became too hard, I shut all my feelings down without knowing it.

Stuffing feelings and pretending like they aren't there doesn't resolve them. The pain stays inside until we deal with it.

The Best Advice

I met my youth pastor, Jim, when I was about 14. This youth pastor changed the whole trajectory of my life. One Sunday, he had invited me to youth group. I was a little reluctant to go because I was afraid of not fitting in, or worse yet, feeling rejected. He reassured me, and I decided to go.

Pastor Jim gave me a ride to youth group each week. We had plenty of long talks on our trips to and from. He talked to me about important things in life. He really cared for and listened to me. Pastor Jim prepared me for the world ahead.

The talk that made the biggest impact on my life was about what to look for in a husband. He explained that if I wasn't careful, I would have a tendency to choose a man who was like the father figures that I grew up with. He talked to me about the propensity for people to repeat what they are used to, perpetuating dysfunctional patterns.

He advised me to write two lists. One contained characteristics that I did NOT want in a husband and the other itemized characteristics that I DID want in my future mate.

He said, "Every time you are deciding whether or not to enter into a relationship, look at your list."

He added, "If the person you are considering is not someone you would want to spend the rest of your life with, then you probably shouldn't be in a relationship with them at all."

This sound advice became my gauge for any future relationships. It protected me from getting into trouble with the wrong people. When I used Pastor Jim's advice to find my husband, I mentally checked my two lists. Those checklists helped me make a vastly different decision than I would have if I didn't have my checklists to go by. My husband Mark is quite different from the father figures I grew up with. My marriage was one of the things that broke generational patterns in my family line.

Sometimes, just recognizing destructive patterns to watch for and guard against can break generational dysfunction. As Pastor Jim talked to me that day, he helped me recognize the sequence I needed to avoid in order to set me on a better path in life. Simply learning about these truths caused me to go in a different direction.

Becoming an Adult

After high school, I moved away to college. Struggling through college to support myself by working long hours, I felt like I had nobody to lean on. Emotionally and financially, I was going through so many life changes. I felt like I did not have anyone to teach me how to meet the challenges successfully.

Pain and problems from childhood followed me as I became an independent adult. I felt insecure about who I was and what I was going to be able to accomplish. Not having the support or encouragement from a parent made me unsure that I could be successful. In addition, not having anyone to teach me structure, time management and self-discipline made it hard to navigate the new responsibilities of college and adult life.

I felt very much alone, even though I had a lot of friends. My friends couldn't give me the support I needed because they were busy becoming adults too. It seemed like everybody else had at least one parent that they could lean on.

I leaned on God with everything in me, but I didn't know how to apply biblical principles to solve my problems. I went to a Christian college but that didn't protect me from getting bombarded with things that shook my faith. Philosophy class messed with my head. This class made me question what I believed and why I believed it. It caused all those solid teachings I had gathered growing up in church to come crashing down. I didn't know what I believed anymore.

All I wanted at this point, was stability. I figured the only way to get that was to find my husband and start a family. I wanted so badly to feel a sense of closeness and stability. I was sure that finding a husband was going to solve all of my problems.

Finding My Husband

Even though I was eager to find my husband, I still evaluated carefully before committing to a man and giving my heart away. I was waiting tables at Denny's during the overnight shift several days a week. Mark came into Denny's one night with a group of business partners and began talking to me. He continued to come in night after night and repeatedly asked me to go on dates with him. He was very persistent and wouldn't take "no" for an answer.

One night, he told me that he was a runner and asked me if I would go running with him. Later, I found out that he'd overheard my conversation with another customer that I was a runner. He used that inside information to lure me into meeting him for a run around the college track. I contemplated carefully and figured it wouldn't hurt. After all, we'd be out in public, and it's not like a "typical date." The following day, he showed up at the track in a pair of high top basketball sneakers. I knew right then and there that he wasn't a runner and that he REALLY wanted to get to know me and would take extreme measures to make it happen. I figured with that kind of tenacity, I needed to give this guy a shot.

Our relationship advanced quickly. We got married in less than a year and had a baby right away. We didn't know each other well, and I was still young. Nobody in our family thought that our marriage (under these circumstances) would last, but we were determined to make it so.

A Rocky Start

Mark and I both came from dysfunctional homes, so we each brought baggage and wounds into our marriage. This made it difficult to establish a healthy new start. We fought all the time about everything. We also found it extremely difficult to be the parents we wanted to be. I knew I wanted our home to be peaceful, loving, and stable, but it was the opposite. The pain from my past triggered the pain from my husband's past and caused us to fight constantly. The anger from childhood pain came out onto my children and husband. We lived in chaos. I wanted to be loving, nurturing and fun, but I was still miserable inside. It was keeping me from being the wife, mother and person I wanted to be.

It was like what Paul said in Romans 7:19 NLT, "I want to do what is good, but I don't. I don't want to do what is wrong, but I do it anyway."

Why couldn't I be the type of mother that I saw at church when I was a little girl? Why was I so angry? Why did I have to control everything and everyone? Why was it so hard to talk to my children and my husband lovingly? I felt like a failure and a bad person.

Victory In the End

As I gained healing, I realized that the people who hurt me as a child were doing so because that's all they knew. They were broken vessels. They were acting out of their hurts and wounds, and they were carrying on the behavioral patterns they learned. Until we recognize the patterns of dysfunction and break them, the behavior will keep moving from generation to generation.

My upbringing had everything to do with how I parented. It affected so many areas. I will share with you how it impacted my family, chapter by chapter.

Breaking free from the hurts of my past has been a process. I struggled with the effects of my childhood until well into adulthood. I went to counseling, emotional healing classes, and all sorts of programs to try to gain victory in my life. The biblical principles taught through Living Waters Ministry with Lee & Denise Boggs, helped me gain the deepest level of healing from the pain of my past. I can tell you that I am not the same person today as I was back then. Through prayer, people, and resources, God has brought me to a place of healing, peace and wholeness.

In these following chapters, I will teach you, step-by-step, how to overcome your past. If I did it, you can do it too.

CHAPTER 2

KNOW YOUR
DESIRED DESTINATION

If you're anything like me, I use a GPS whenever I venture outside my familiar surroundings. Before going anywhere, I need to enter my desired destination into the device. Parenting can be the same way. You need to know where you want to end up to get to your destination. So let me ask you, do you know where you want your family to arrive in life? What does your goal look like on your journey to a better, happier family?

I had a vision for my family. I knew I wanted things to be different from the family I grew up in, but I didn't know how to get there. So, as you define where you want to end up, you can then use the principles we talk about in this book as your own GPS.

When I went to church as a little girl and observed godly families, I saw the characteristics that I wanted in my own family when I got older. I wanted my family to be happy, stable, loving, and close-knit. But because I didn't have the example to guide me, I prayed that God would give me the tools, resources, and people to lead me along my journey.

The Way God Intended Home To Be

From the beginning, God intended for parents to be representative of His love to their children. As parents know God's love and express His love, children know and feel God's love.

God's love is unconditional, perfect, and without limits. God loves us just because we are His. We don't have to work, strive, or earn His love. Unconditional means you don't have to meet certain conditions.

Did you feel loved unconditionally in childhood, or did you feel like you had to earn it?

For me, I felt loved if I did all my chores, was helpful around the house, earned good grades in school, always agreed with what my mother said, and did everything right.

A conditional kind of love sets our hearts up for a performance mentality and perfectionism. Unfortunately, this type of love also causes more wounds and hurts.

My life as a child was built around making sure I did enough work and was "good enough" to be loved. This kind of mentality translated into adulthood as well. As I became an adult, I felt like I could never say "no" to anyone. I had to always say "yes" so that I would be accepted. This kind of life is exhausting, always needing to work to be accepted. Until I gained healing, I didn't feel like I could ever be good enough. Most times, perfectionism kept me from even trying to start projects, fearing that it wouldn't be perfect and thus not being good enough. Do you feel like you have to work to be accepted and loved?

This is not how God wants us to live, always working to earn our value. God's love is unconditional and can't be compared to an imperfect parent's conditional love. Because our parents were supposed to represent

God's love, without even knowing it, we measure God's love by how our parents loved us. We need to understand that we are valued and loved by God, no matter what. Once this becomes our reality, we can then live a life of freedom.

If you had to earn love from your parents, you might feel like you have to earn God's love. If you learned conditional love from childhood, you probably are giving conditional love as a parent. The only way to learn God's kind of love, if this wasn't what you experienced as a child, is to spend time with Him. As you spend time with God (in prayer and scripture), you'll understand His love and character and, therefore, will be able to represent it to your child. When parents know and communicate this unconditional love, children feel wholly accepted, valued, and secure. However, suppose a child feels that there are conditions to be met in order to be loved and accepted. In that case, they will struggle to thrive emotionally, spiritually, and developmentally.

Nurture, acceptance, and encouragement are as essential to our soul as food, water, and shelter are to our bodies. When we go without food and water, our physical bodies begin to die. The same thing happens to our souls. As we go without the proper love and emotional needs, we start to die on the inside.

What kind of love did you experience in childhood? How does this affect your household?

Definition of Love

We can learn a lot about how to truly love our children by practicing and teaching the words found at 1 Corinthians 13:4-7 NLT. It defines love like this: *"Love is patient and kind. Love is not jealous or boastful or proud or rude. It does not demand its own way. It is not irritable, and it keeps no record of being wronged. It does not rejoice about injustice but rejoices whenever the truth wins out. Love never gives up, never loses faith, is always hopeful, and endures through every circumstance."*

Let's take a closer look at this scripture. According to this, if we love our children God's way we will be *patient* and *kind* to them. I know this is easier said than done sometimes, especially when they act in ways that try our patience and kindness.

Love is not proud. I had to learn how to apologize to my kids and admit my mistakes. When I did this, I noticed that it helped me get my attitude straight regarding my kids. When we humble ourselves enough to admit when we are wrong, it allows God to come into the situation to change us. The other thing I noticed is that it helps build a better relationship with our kids because we've come down to a level that they can relate to and identify with. We are no longer raising ourselves above them but showing that they are just as important. We are admitting that we, too, have an authority to answer to—God! This lets our children know that it's okay to make mistakes and shows them how to fix them. We admit our wrongs and then clean up our messes. In those moments when I yelled at my child and knew I had blown it, I apologized and made it right.

Love is not rude. This means we need to respect our children, even though they are little people. We, as parents, can be rude to our children with our tone and actions, especially if they are being difficult. But love will cause us to modify our response and replace rudeness with love.

Love is not irritable. This can be hard when we are tired or frustrated.

Irritability comes out in our attitude towards our children. It undermines a peaceful atmosphere in our house. It's also challenging to get our children to respond positively to anything we say or do when our underlying mood is irritable. Excessive irritability can also feel like a form of rejection to our children (Ephesians 6:4).

Love does not keep a record of being wronged. When our children need discipline, we correct them, forgive them, and then wipe the slate clean. However, sometimes we can detect a particular attitude or pattern of behavior in one of our children. Then we can find ourselves watching for the bad. We want to clear the slate and be sure we are watching for the good, in order to encourage our children and not anticipate their faults.

Love never gives up, never loses faith, is always hopeful, and endures through every circumstance. We never give up on our kids. We never lose faith in what God is doing in them through us. We always endure. We continue to persevere in all that comes with parenting, even in those tough times. I see parents drop the ball and give in to inappropriate behavior in their children because it's easier to walk away than it is to deal with it. If we give up when things look impossible, we will never get the reward of seeing our kids achieve their fullest potential. God never gives up on us. He has faith in us, and sees us through, also helping our children make it through those tough times as well.

Suppose we can follow this guideline of loving our children. In that case, it'll make it so much easier to establish these principles in our children. Modeling this love structure in our lives helps us have a basis to then teach our children how to respond to each other. This passage is an excellent guideline and reference of acceptable behavior when strife, quarreling, and conflict arise in the family.

Growing Fruit

God used my garden to teach me a lesson about nurturing and loving my children in order to help them grow good fruit and be healthy, happy, and stable. We moved from New York, where the soil is rich and soft, to South Carolina, where the ground is hard and clay-like. I'd been trying to modify the soil so we can grow some of our favorite foods.

One year, I grew my plants in pots so that I could control the soil contents better. Weeks went by, and I got excited because I saw flowers on my tomato plants. Another week went by, and these flowers looked pretty, but they didn't produce fruit. I didn't care if my tomato plants looked pretty, I wanted fruit. I wanted to eat some fresh tomatoes.

I read somewhere that if I wanted my tomato plants to grow more fruit and less excessive foliage, I could feed them plant food. Apparently, plant food gives plants the nutrients to help them be productive and grow fruit like they're supposed to. So I put the plant food on my plants, and sure enough, they started producing tomatoes.

Picture this: the child is like the tomato plant, and you are the pot of soil that your child grows in. Suppose we do not have the nutrients in our soil because our childhood was depleted of the emotional nutrients and love we needed. In that case, we need to enrich the soil of our homes to grow healthy children. Along with the necessary nutrients in the soil of our homes, the soil needs to be evaluated for toxins, ph levels, and weeds that could further stifle the development of our children. If you, as a parent, grew up in a home where the soil was void of emotional nutrients, your "parenting soil" will be deficient as well and probably contain toxins and weeds. To truly grow healthy children, we need to check the soil of our homes to create an environment where we can grow healthy, happy children that produce good fruit.

We can make sure our soil is rich in nutrients by diving into God's word and spending quiet time with our Heavenly Father daily. Furthermore, we need to go through a process of healing and changing the environment of our soil by removing the toxins and correcting the deficiencies. When we parent with emotional deficiency, it creates a potentially volatile environment, which we will discuss in the upcoming chapters.

Safe and Stable

Our home should be a safe and stable environment. We can create this type of environment in a few different ways.

Establish unconditional love. Unconditional love needs to be the foundation of each relationship in the home, especially from parent to child. This kind of love is without conditions, it is not self-seeking, does not expect anything in return. 1 Corinthians 13 is a good model to teach and follow.

Establishing risk-free communication. Part of creating a stable home is through communication: spouse-to-spouse, parent-to-child, and child-to-parent, without fear of rejection or invalidation. Communication is vital in creating a safe home. Model safety by apologizing and admitting when you, as the parent, exhibit wrong behavior. You can use it as a teaching moment by explaining feelings, why, and what happened as your emotions were out of control. Being vulnerable and honest with your children helps them feel safe with you.

Establishing trust. Trust is established when each part of the family can share their thoughts, feelings, emotions, and opinions without fearing an overreaction or harsh response from the other person.

Ability to express feelings. Children have feelings and emotions but many times they don't understand how to process what they are feeling. A safe home allows children to show feelings and emotions without shutting them down via invalidating words or reactions. It is important to allow children to express their feelings and then validate their feelings by talking with them.

Start Building Stability

As we go through the following chapters, we will talk about roadblocks and challenges that can hinder the process of establishing a safe place in your home. Over this next week, you can begin taking steps towards making your home a healthier environment by exercising communication each day. Each night before bed, I suggest incorporating time to talk about the day. During this time, you can ask your child, using age-appropriate language, if anything happened that day that made them feel bad. As the parent, you need to be prepared and positioned not to get angry or defensive regardless of the child's response. Your child needs to feel safe sharing his or her thoughts and feelings. As your child shares feelings, let them talk until they are done, and then you can share positive, loving, and encouraging words in response. This is not a time for correction but a connection with your child. Each day journal your child's response and your response to the child to watch as your relationship begins to grow closer.

Write Your Vision

What are the changes you want to see in your family? Do you see fruit in your behavior that you need to change? Are there areas where you and your spouse interact that need to change?

Identify those areas in parenting that are not producing good fruit. Take some time to write down the vision you see for your household.

It doesn't matter how you write it, as long as you write it. Writing your vision and goals on paper will allow you to narrow down your final destination and how you want your family to be. It will create a clear path. As you write it down, ask God to give you clarity, strength, and courage to do the things that will help you become the parent you want to be and that God wants you to be.

In order to respond to your child with God's type of love, you need to allow God to heal and change your heart. I pray that God uses this book as the roadmap along your journey to healing and better parenting.

CHAPTER 3

GOING BACK TO MOVE FORWARD

As I entered into parenthood, why was I not able to parent the way I wanted to? I knew exactly the type of parent I wanted to be, but my parenting reality always fell short no matter how hard I tried. As you can tell by my story, I didn't have that solid example I needed to become a functional parent. I was not naturally given what was necessary to be able to give my children what they needed.

Maybe you can relate to some of my story. Have you ever heard of the phrase "Hurt people, hurt people?" It's so true. I had pain and wounds from my childhood that were being projected onto the people I loved most. Even though I didn't want to hurt people, especially my children, I did it unintentionally. When we have wounds from an imperfect past, triggers will generate hurtful responses coming from our own hurt. On top of the triggers, we can also respond to our spouse and children with coping mechanisms that push them away or isolate ourselves in an attempt to keep us "safe" from getting hurt again. The problem is that those trigger responses negatively affect the people around us, especially the people that we are closest to. Much of these triggered responses can be traced back to pain and a lack of the basic emotional needs in our childhood. I first learned about these unmet emotional needs and how they affect parenting and present-day situations when I attended a retreat at Living Waters Ministry in Hiddenite, North Carolina. This realization has changed every aspect of how I deal with my children, husband, and others.

What was your home like growing up? Were you like me, dealing with a lot of dysfunction, or did you have a pretty good childhood?

Let's face it, we all grew up in less than perfect homes. No parent is perfect. Even after going through healing and being aware of my imperfections, I can still be better each day as a mother. Recognizing where our parents could have done better allows us an advantage: to rise to a higher level of parenting.

A "dysfunctional family" can be defined as one or both parents not acting in a fully functional role as parent or not filling all of a child's emotional needs.

Referring to my analogy in the last chapter about my tomato plants, was the soil of your home growing up full of nutrients or was it lacking? In childhood, were you grown in the rich soil of love, supplying you with the nutrients that satisfied all of your emotional needs? God gave every human on Earth emotional needs that are as essential to our souls as our natural needs are to our bodies. If you didn't get these emotional needs met, your soul will crave them just like your body craves food when you are hungry and water when you are thirsty. Just like you can get grumpy when you lack food, you can get angry when you lack love.

Deficits of love and emotional needs in childhood can dramatically affect how you perceive life and function in relationships and parenting later on. Our negative behaviors in parenting often stem from this deficit. These emotional needs are a measurement of how loved you felt as a child. If your parents met your needs in childhood, it gave you a foundation for adulthood and parenthood.

As you go through this next section, think about how full the soil of your heart was for each of these categories growing up. Was it fertile soil where love could grow and give good fruit or stony soil where only weeds and hurt grew? I'm not talking about occasionally when your parents were happy and everything seemed good, but on a daily basis.

Evaluating

I'm going to use my story to show you how the lack of emotional needs affected me as a child and into parenthood. As we go along, I want you to evaluate your childhood. Think of the soil of your heart. As we go through our stories, it is not to determine where our parents failed or to say they were bad people. Instead, it gives us a clue into evaluating how yesterday is impacting today. Suppose by going through this chapter you realize that you didn't get your needs met as a child. Don't worry. In that case, we will work through how to process this information as we go through the healing journey together, chapter by chapter.

Recognizing that we all have a need to be loved, nurtured, and accepted is one of the first steps to gaining healing and victory. Many times we try to fill those empty places in our hearts with the wrong things. As we move forward, we will learn how to recognize the deficits and also realize the proper way to fill them.

Evaluating the emptiness in our souls and deficits of our emotional needs is like going to the doctor for our physical check-ups. To figure out what's going on in your physical health, the doctor asks questions and check the symptoms you're experiencing. When evaluating our soul, we need to do the same thing to gauge the health of our emotional wellbeing.

Did You Feel Approval?

The foundation of our emotional stability is to be completely accepted and have approval from the two most significant people in our lives: our parents. Did you feel accepted by your parents, even if you brought home bad grades or messed up? Approval is the opposite of rejection. Suppose your parents accepted you just how God made you. In that case, you knew you were loved and valued without feeling insecure about who you were. If you struggled with the abandonment of a parent, emotionally or physically, you probably struggled to feel accepted in childhood as well as in adulthood.

We all have a need for approval no matter what, regardless of mistakes we've made-good or bad grades, boy or girl, skilled or not at sports, compliant or mischievous.

For me, there was always an underlying feeling of not being accepted. I knew that I was the result of an unplanned pregnancy. My mother was the provider of our family and did not want the burden of another child. My older sister was eight years older when my mother conceived me, so she was well past "baby mode." As a result, there was always a "conditional" love. I had to be compliant and agreeable. If I wasn't, I was harshly punished and shunned from my parents' positive attention or love. My mother reminded me regularly that she had to work to the bone to provide for us which made me feel like a burden.

As an adult, I felt a need to perform and "people-please" to feel accepted and loved by others. I also struggled with poor self-image, insecurity, and feelings of rejection. Consequently, I believed that I would never be good enough, and I needed to work harder in order to be valued.

As an adult, do you struggle with trying to earn value or love, people-pleasing, workaholicism, low self-worth, insecurity, defensiveness, and feeling rejected?

As a parent, if you did not feel the approval from your parents in child-hood, you could be guarded and unintentionally keep your child at a distance today. Additionally, you could possibly be pushing them away.

I wanted to feel accepted so badly that I thought indeed having children would satisfy this need. When our children rely on us for everything, we feel wanted and needed. Their reliance on us fills our need for acceptance temporarily until they become more independent. As soon as my children became more independent, it triggered a feeling of rejection inside me, and I began to guard my heart. As I guarded my heart, my children felt me pulling back, making them feel a restriction of love.

The deficit of this need has such a massive impact on our lives. The enemy uses rejection so strategically to destroy lives and to disrupt God's purpose for your life. Rejection is an attack on who God created you to be. I will talk more about rejection and its impact on parenting in the next chapter.

As a child, did you feel acceptance and approval by your mom and dad? How does this affect your life today?

Were You Nurtured?

As a child, you needed your parents to spend quality time with you, making you feel special, loved, and valued. Interaction between you and your parents-when they listened, cuddled, played with you, and comforted you-let you know you were loved and significant. Hugs, kisses, and attention added deposits of love into the soil of your heart.

Do you feel like your parents spent quality time with you? Did they make you feel important by showing interest in you and the things you found important? Did you get hugs, kisses, or a comforting touch from Mom and Dad?

We followed the rule that "children should be seen and not heard" in my home, and I felt invisible. By the age of four, I was fatherless and my mother was either working or too busy to pay attention to me. I felt lonely a lot. I tried hard to lay low and fly under the radar. The attention that we got in our household was negative. My siblings acted out and were rebellious to gain any attention they could. I preferred to keep the peace .

As I shared with you in the first chapter, I gained attention by competing in pageants. Being on stage and competing created an opportunity to gain attention from my mother and others. As a result, I became addicted to performing. I also realized that if I looked pretty I could gain attention from the opposite gender. What did you do to get attention?

As an adult, I was consumed with my appearance and making sure I looked good. I believed the lie that this was the only way I could gain acceptance and attention from people. I performed in everything I did. I had to be the best at everything, and I worked harder than anyone around me to gain attention and value. I had a low self-image and felt like I could never measure up.

Did you have to earn attention (sports, good grades, being funny) growing up?

In parenting, the lack of attention and affirmation in my childhood fueled my "perfectionist" mindset toward the expectations of my children. The attention I gave my children was based on them excelling at something. I was not given attention as a child, so I didn't know how to give it to my children. I thought that I gave them the attention they needed, but I realized that it was conditional. I never had an adult play with me or spend time with me as a young child, so it was hard to relate to my children on their level to give them the attention they needed daily.

Not having a father present and a mother that did not know how to nurture, I was raised in a home where appropriate affection did not exist. The only time I received nurturing as a kid was during a brief time when I went for weekend visits to my great-grandparents' house. They made me feel special. I cuddled on their laps, and they gave me plenty of hugs and kisses. As my mother took me away from them, I could feel the void in my life and struggled to feel loved.

On the other hand, the nurturing that I did receive as a child was inappropriate. My father sexually abused me before he left our home. This abuse significantly affected my marriage and parenting. I suppressed my memories of this until several years into my marriage. I had a tough time with any sort of closeness or intimacy with my husband. For the longest time, I felt ashamed and dirty. As an adult, I have struggled with receiving or giving affection. My triggered responses caused issues with my husband and my children feeling loved by me. As a result of not having this need met in my life, I grew into adulthood guarded and distant from people in general. I found it hard to have close relationships. I didn't know how to have closeness with others, and it felt unnatural.

When a person receives inappropriate physical touch as a child, it not only leaves the void of the right kind of love, but it perverts their expectation of it. People that have been sexually abused or touched inappropriately tend to go from one extreme to another in adulthood. They can either be distant and guarded (not wanting affection) or promiscuous and need excessive sexual affection.

Because of the inappropriate physical affection I received as a child, it was challenging for me to respond to my husband's love when we got married. I couldn't believe that my husband's love didn't have strings attached. This cycle made it hard to receive affection in any way.

In parenting, it was hard to nurture my children after they reached about two years old, due to the sexual abuse I endured and not having appropriate nurturing growing up. I remember sitting on the couch with my children, and if they sat too close to me, I felt suffocated. Lack of affection and nurturing towards my children communicated to them that I was rejecting them, causing them to feel unloved.

As I grew into adulthood, I believed that I was unlovable and something was wrong with me. Suppose you did not get the nurturing you needed. In that case, you may excuse it with, "Oh, we just weren't that kind of family." Many people think that if you didn't grow up with hugs and kisses from mom and dad, that it was normal and just how it was supposed to be. This is not true. God made us all with the need to be nurtured, and if you didn't get it in childhood, you could interpret it as being unloved and rejected.

Did you have someone to nurture you when you were hurting? As a child, you needed someone to comfort you in times of emotional or physical pain.

Suppose you didn't receive comfort as a child. In that case, you could have a hard time comforting your own children or others around you. To the other extreme, you could feel the need to fix everyone and everything around you. If you weren't nurtured or comforted in childhood, this could also cause you to feel lonely, empty, or numb as an adult.

Here's an example: A child falls off his bike and scrapes his knee. The child needs someone to pick him up, speak comforting words, and take care of his wounds with gentleness and nurturing. The opposite of comforting would be for the parent to scold the boy and say things like,

"Boys don't cry, so stop crying," or, "Wipe the dirt off and keep going," or, "You're alright, it doesn't hurt that bad."

Did you feel that you were nurtured in childhood? How is this affecting your parenting today? Are you able to nurture, comfort, and hug your children? Are you able to spend quality time with your child (playing with them, talking with them, entering into their world)?

Were You Encouraged?

Encouragement is giving someone support, confidence, or hope. Your parents needed to recognize your positive attributes and strengths as they inspired and encouraged you to accomplish goals and achievements by verbal declarations of affirmation. Encouragement helps you develop the gifts that God placed within you.

Verbal affirmation is a vital form of encouragement. It helps you, as the child, know you have value. When your parent tells you the good traits in your character and your abilities, you become aware of who God created you to be. As a child, did your parents tell you they were proud of you (for who you are as an individual)? Did your parents call out and define your natural God-given strengths?

The father has the most vital voice to speak into the child's identity. If your father was either missing or not functioning in his role, the result is that you can grow up not knowing who you are or what you were born to do. It makes it extremely hard to succeed if this is the case. Suppose you didn't have the affirmation you needed in childhood. In that case, you can feel like you are wandering around in life, not knowing where you belong or where you are going.

Contrarily, suppose your parents gave negative affirmation instead of positive. In that case, it created a deficit of this emotional need. It compounded the issues by directly attacking your value as a person. For example, if a father says, "You'll never amount to anything," or "You're a crybaby," or anything condescending, it can cause significant damage to your identity. A child will believe whatever negative words are being directed at them. This belief will cause the person to get stuck in unsuccessful patterns in life as an adult. Without knowing it, if you didn't receive verbal reassurance in your childhood, it created a feeling of low self-worth that you can then, as a parent, project onto your child.

As a teenager, my step-father actively tore down my self-worth and my identity. He said things to me that would make me feel dirty and ashamed. As a good Christian girl, I tried to live a life of strict purity with my actions, dress, and words. I was incredibly careful not to act promiscuously. He called me names that would insinuate that I was soliciting myself to men. He continually accused me, twisted my actions, and questioned my motives to make me believe that I was dirty and shameful.

The accusing words of my step-father were devastating. They caused me to question my identity. Because I was raised in such a dysfunctional home, any bit of identity that I could gain from my faith was destroyed. The enemy used him to attack my Christian values, the only thing that was building my worth, value, and identity.

As if being a teen wasn't hard enough, my "father figure" told me things that made me feel self-conscience and increasingly awkward. The enemy knew precisely how to discourage me and challenge my faith in myself and in God. His relentless verbal abuse—in the form of sexual accusations—also triggered the shame and pain of being sexually abused. His negative affirmation wrecked my identity and self-image.

Consequently, I entered into adulthood and parenthood feeling defeated, shameful, and worthless. In parenting, if you don't know your own identity, purpose, and value, it's hard to instill that in your children. Because we can't recognize our self-worth, it's challenging to recognize the gifts, unique traits, and innate value in our children. Also, when you don't feel good about yourself, it's harder to encourage others (including your children).

As you reached your preteen and teen years, encouragement was essential in helping you have confidence in achieving success. Encouragement is given through affirming words about your abilities and your parents' confidence in you to accomplish great things. As parents encourage their children, they help them learn to create structured plans to achieve what they set out to do.

Teenagers need emotional support and encouragement to help assist them through difficult situations. Suppose you didn't feel supported by your parents when you were trying to accomplish an objective. In that case, you could give up before accomplishing your goal. A repetitive cycle of this happening could cause you to believe you're a failure, incapable of success.

As I started college, I realized my need for emotional support was lacking. As I saw my friends with parents to lean on, I felt all alone. The transition to college was a challenging season in my life as it seemed scary and so different. I felt like I had the weight of the world on my shoulders and no one to help me hold it. Things were changing so quickly that I longed for someone to lean on.

Another example of support in childhood would be your parent sitting beside you to help with a school project or help you come to a resolution with a friend or a sibling.

As an adult, do you experience confusion, the need to "people-please," discouragement, defeat, frustration, lack of confidence, fear of failure, timidity, and insecurity? These symptoms may be the result of not receiving support and encouragement in childhood.

Do you see how a deficit of encouragement and support in the "soil of your home" may be affecting your parenting today?

Did You Feel Stable?

Growing up, was your home stable? Was your home peaceful or was there a lot of fighting? Did your parents have reasonable rules and comparable consequences if those rules were broken? Did your parents protect you?

Stability is to feel safe and secure, knowing that your physical, emotional, and provisional needs will be met. If you did not have safety and security, you probably didn't feel stable. Consequently, if you grew up not feeling stable, you could be trying to create stability by attempting to control everything. Suppose you grew up in a home that did not meet your needs monetarily. In that case, you could deal with feeling insecure about being provided for as an adult.

As I shared in the first chapter, there was a lot of physical and verbal abuse in my childhood. I did not feel safe or secure as a child.

The rules in my household were constantly changing. I didn't know what to expect or how to live up to my parents' expectations. I dealt with fear, worry, and insecurity as a child and into my adulthood. As I became a young adult and into adulthood, I started to feel like I needed to control people, situations, and my environment. I controlled my children, my husband, and the orderliness of my home and my life. I needed to plan everything, and everything had to be clean and orderly for me to feel safe and secure and not feel like my life was going to fall apart. Also, due to my need to control everything, I had a hard time surrendering situations in my life to God and believing Him to take care of me. Was your home stable? If not, how is this affecting your household now?

Were You Valued?

You learned that you were important and worthy by how the significant people in your life treated you. Respect and appreciation communicate value to a child, especially to a preteen or a teenager.

Appreciation is recognizing the good qualities in you or something you did. Furthermore, whether with words or actions, your parents communicate your worth, quality, or importance to them. When parents focus on the good things children do and on their accomplishments, without nitpicking the things they do wrong, kids feel appreciated.

From the time I was nine years old until I left home, I had excessive chores and a heavy workload. The responsibilities I carried were far above what was age-appropriate. I was rarely able to have fun with friends because I first had to have all my chores completed, which was almost impossible. I felt unappreciated. There were never any words spoken that communicated appreciation. Still, I always needed to try harder and harder to please my mother and step-father. The only feedback I received from my hard work was either that something was wrong or that another job was added to my list. The lack of appreciation I grew up with caused me to believe that I always had to work harder to gain love and worth.

Without knowing it, my constant working and striving carried over into parenting. I expected my children to work harder, communicating that if it wasn't perfect, it wasn't good enough. As a result, my perfectionist mentality caused my children to feel discouraged and give up on things. The deficit of appreciation causes an inability to believe that you can do a good job. As perfectionism takes over, you think your best is never good enough, and it creates a fear of failure. It can be such an intense fear of not being good enough that it can make a person reluctant to initiate a project, let alone finish one.

Suppose you did not feel appreciated in childhood. In that case, you may find that you are discouraged easily, pessimistic or insecure as an adult. You may also believe, "I'll never be able to be successful," "I'm not good enough," or "I'm not important."

Growing up, did you feel appreciated?

Respect is another way value and worth are communicated to a child. It's having regard for a child's rights, feelings, and sense of belongings. Respect is shown by tone of voice and honoring boundaries.

I remember always being talked to in a tone and words that were demeaning. I got the impression growing up that I wasn't as important as the adults. There was a sense that children didn't matter as much as parents, nor did their thoughts, opinions, privacy, or possessions. My mother or step-father would come into my room and search it at any point and throw my things around like they didn't have value. As I was treated like I was less important, I believed that I was. This feeling carried over into adult life situations.

If you were not respected as a child, you may feel worthless, inferior, insecure, or demanding as an adult. As a parent, you could project your deficit of respect in childhood onto your children, possibly harshly demanding respect from them but not modeling first.

Growing up, did you receive respect as a person or for your privacy and property?

How has a deficit of appreciation or respect affected your parenting?

Life With a Deficit

In any of these areas, having a lack in childhood contributes to relationship problems, emotional pain, rejection, and negative behaviors we experience as adults. A deficit in any of these areas will also cause you to have a parental handicap. If you do not deal with your deficiencies they will continue to affect your children and be handed down to yet another generation.

Living in Denial

If you didn't have the needs I outlined previously met as a child, maybe you're thinking the same thing I did: I don't need anything from anyone. When you go through life needing something, and go long enough without getting it, it hurts to even expect it anymore. When failed expectations pile up and it hurts too much to expect the needs to be filled, sometimes people start denying that they have needs at all. God made us with emotional needs and denying that we need them will not make the needs go away. It would be like saying that a plant doesn't need water anymore after enduring a drought. The plant needs water as much as our soul needs our emotional needs met.

Since I had very little of my emotional needs met as a child, I learned quickly that I couldn't rely on anyone. At a very young age, I remember convincing myself that I needed to be self-reliant and shut people out. I believed that if I didn't rely on anyone, I could avoid being a burden. This pattern kept everyone blocked out of my life (including my children) and kept God out as well. As I functioned out of self-reliance, it kept my husband from stepping into his God-given role in our family. My self-sufficiency put my husband in a box that would not let him assume any of the responsibilities pertaining to our family. Self-reliance communicated to my husband and children that my husband was incompetent and it blocked him from being the priest and leader of our household.

Holes In the Cup

One day, as I was ministering to a woman (we'll call her Cindy), I had a vision. I held a cup in my hand to represent a measurement of the love she received as a little girl. In my spiritual minds-eye, I saw holes in the bottom of the cup.

Cindy grew up in a home that fulfilled her natural needs but very little of her emotional needs. She had to meet requirements before she felt accepted and affirmed. Cindy had to achieve straight A's in school, play the sports her dad wanted her to, clean her room just right, never make too much noise, and always be agreeable. She felt like she had to be perfect in hopes of measuring up to the standards of her parents. The pain she experienced as a child, not feeling accepted for who she was, caused her heart to have holes in it as an adult.

Now, as a mother and wife, she still felt the pain and emptiness of her past. She looked to all the wrong things to fill her needs: shopping, eating, Netflix, and people-pleasing, to help her feel better. In order to feel fulfilled, she worked hard to check off her daily list: serve in church, pray and read her Bible. Yet she still felt empty and had nothing to pour into her family.

I then saw in the vision that as she sat in God's presence, not just to meet daily requirements but to genuinely seek a relationship with Him, the holes in her cup began to seal up by God's love. As she consistently allowed God to fill her heart with His love, the holes sealed up more and more. The more consistently she experienced God's love and approval, the fuller she became, and it was then that her cup began to overflow. As this happened, she could then overflow into her children, husband, and those around her.

In Jeremiah 2:11-13 God says, *"11 Has a nation [ever] changed gods even though they were not gods [but merely man-made objects]? But My people have exchanged their Glory (the true God) For that [man-made idol] which does not benefit [them]. 12 Be appalled, O heavens, at this; Be shocked and shudder with horror [at the behavior of the people]," says the Lord. 13 For My people have committed two evils: They have abandoned (rejected) Me, The fountain of living water, And they have carved out their own cisterns, Broken cisterns That cannot hold water. "*

As the Israelites did in this scripture, we often look to other things besides God to fill our needs and make us feel better. The problem with this is, none of the worldly things we choose to fill our voids with can seal the holes in our soul, heal us or truly fulfill us. We end up as empty and broken vessels.

God chose parents as the vessels to pour His love into us as His children. If we don't position ourselves to be sealed up, healed up, and then filled up from the only true source, we will have nothing left to pour into our children.

In creating that safe and loving environment for our children, we need to make sure we spend time with God daily. I'll share more about this in the upcoming chapters.

CHAPTER 4

BREAKING THE PATTERNS

The pain of our past and the deficit of emotional needs in childhood contribute greatly to keeping us stuck in unsuccessful parenting cycles. Our past pain causes us to produce behaviors that are considered "bad fruit" in our lives. We can get stuck in the process of trying to protect ourselves from more hurt and dealing with the pain we already have. The ways we deal with pain come from defensive behavior, walls, addictions, triggers, projecting pain onto others, and wearing masks to keep people from truly knowing who we are.

Emotional wounds are like toxins and weeds planted in the soil of our hearts. The weeds germinate, grow, and take root. And each weed has many different roots that cause it to lodge tightly in the soil of our hearts. To gain freedom from the effects of past pain, we need to intentionally uproot the weeds from the garden of our hearts. If the weeds of hurt are left unattended, the pain in our hearts continues to grow, and over time, causes us to form a hardened heart. The Bible describes this as a heart of stone in Ezekiel 36:26 and Matthew 13. Out of the response to pain and not wanting to be hurt the same way again, we form walls around our heart. Each painful situation represents a hardened area in this wall of protection. One area at a time, this wall of protection blocks you in and keeps others out. You may not even be aware that you're building a wall. Still, it becomes apparent later in life when you try building healthy relationships with your spouse, children, and others. As the walls of protection are in place, you can feel lonely and shut off, like you're in a personal prison. With a hardened heart, you may notice symptoms such as guardedness, an inability to be yourself, emotional numbness, continual fear of rejection, an inability to trust others, and the tendency to push people away as they get close to you.

The Wall

Looking back, I realize I started forming a wall around my heart as early as middle school. I noticed it was tough for me to make friends, because I was so afraid of rejection. The more I feared rejection, the more I pretended to be someone else, hoping that people would like that version of me. But as I put on different masks, in attempt to to be someone else, it started to backfire. My peers pushed me away even more. My reality became a constant cycle of rejection. My wounds from childhood caused me to communicate a confusing message to everyone around me. I felt like I had a label on my forehead that told people to reject me. My guarded heart caused me to carry emotional and social handicaps, and it kept me from functioning in all areas of my life. It seemed like anything I put my hands to was unsuccessful. I frequently found myself being misunderstood. People only saw the anger, bitterness, and hardness from the outside, but I was crying out for someone to accept me and love me from the inside. My wounds and walls pushed people away.

My hardened heart also affected my relationship with God. As I tried to get close to God, it seemed like I ran into a brick wall. When I prayed, worshipped, or read my Bible, it seemed like God was ignoring me. It seemed as though God was rejecting me just like everyone else did. I couldn't feel Him or hear Him. Eventually, as I persisted in pursuing God, I realized that it wasn't God's brick wall that I was running into. It was my own. It was the same wall that I built to protect myself from people.

Do you find yourself being guarded? Are you fearful of rejection? Do you feel lonely or isolated? Do you have a hard time connecting in relationships and friendships? Do you have a hard time trusting people? Do you feel like you have no feelings or feel numb?

If you answered yes to one or more of these questions, odds are you've built a wall around your heart, possibly without even knowing it.

Strongholds and Lies

Along with the weeds of worldly pain, the enemy adds toxic lies in the soil of your heart. The enemy's lies cause hurt and pain to grow more and more. Have you ever thought to yourself, "I'm not good enough," "Nobody cares about me," "Nobody likes me," "If they get to know me, they won't like me," or "I'm not wanted"? These are some of the lies that can be planted as we endure painful situations and have unmet needs. When we are young, the enemy plants lies in our hearts to destroy our self-confidence and purpose. These lies keep us from our God-given destiny. Therefore, the enemy starts early in life, when we are young and impressionable, so that he has a greater chance of destroying our hopes and plans before they begin.

The enemy uses the hurts and wounds that affect our soul to form a stronghold over our thinking, affecting our will and emotions. Strongholds are wrong thinking patterns that do not line up with the Word of God.

Definition: Stronghold—1) A place that has been fortified to protect it against attack. 1.1) A place where a particular cause or belief is strongly defended or upheld. (Oxford Advanced Learner's Dictionary)

These lies and strongholds affect the way we believe and behave. Proverbs 23:7 NKJV says, *"For as a man thinks in his heart, so is he."*

Each time you agree with or entertain a lie, the influence of it gets stronger and bigger. The lie becomes more and more your reality as you function like it's your truth. What does it mean to agree with or entertain a lie? It means that you embrace it, accept it, and act as if it was the truth. If you believe you are rejected, you approach new relationships from a position in your heart, mind, and body language of rejection. This positioning of yourself makes you appear guarded and communicates that you are rejecting the people you actually desire acceptance from. As you act guarded, others feel rejected by you and then put their own guards up, ironically making it feel like they are rejecting you. This cycle perpetuates and reinforces your belief that you are rejected.

Self-Sufficiency

Janice grew up in a single-parent household. Her father left when she was five. Janice's mother worked many long hours as she was the only provider of the home. Janice had to grow up quickly and lost out on her childhood as she had to step in and do chores and responsibilities beyond her years. Janice took care of her younger brother when her mother was away.

Janice's mother did not have the physical or emotional energy to give her the attention, nurturing or emotional support that she needed in the evenings. Janice needed her mother to wrap her arms around her, hug her, or let Janice sit on her lap. She needed someone to ask her how her day was, to listen to her, and to give her attention, letting her know she was loved and valued. Her mother provided for her physical needs, but Janice learned that she had nobody to care for her emotional needs. She felt rejected and alone. It hurt too much to rely on someone to meet her needs and continually find them unmet. Little by little, she learned she needed to take care of herself. She grew to be self-sufficient.

Janice's stronghold was that nobody (including God) would take care of her and that she needed to take care of herself. This stronghold blocked anyone that tried to help her. Janice had a hard time praying and believing that God would help her or answer her prayers. She measured God's faithfulness and ability to take care of her by the lack she experienced through her parents-her dad walking out and her mother's inability to connect with her emotionally.

Fast forward fifteen years, Janice got married and couldn't trust her husband to take care of her and wouldn't let him try. Frank, her husband, then couldn't take his God-given place in the family unit as the leader of their household because Janice insisted on taking care of everything. As Janice insisted on taking care of everything, her husband got triggered because he felt that she didn't trust him to do anything and made him feel inferior and not good enough. Her self-sufficiency was the source of a lot of fighting in their marriage. As a mother, Janice's actions communicated to her children that they also needed to grow up to take care of themselves and not rely on others. Also, Janice's stronghold, without knowing it, stunted her children's faith and ability to trust God. Her self-sufficiency blocked the love in her household, both giving and receiving.

Triggers

Triggers are present-day feelings that are affected by the pain of your past. Do you notice yourself overreacting to things and feeling angry for no apparent reason? Do you get your feelings hurt a lot? Do you feel rejected frequently?

These are all symptoms of triggers or indicators that whatever just happened set off the deep-seated pain created by something that happened in your childhood. When feelings trigger us, it gives a clue into what's causing us to respond to things inappropriately (anger, yelling, passivity, isolation, blaming, arguing, or pushing loved ones away). As we feel those feelings, we need to trace the triggers. Tracing the trigger means we acknowledge the feeling in order to find the pain buried in our hearts. The pain is generally linked to one of the areas of unmet needs in childhood or a painful situation that took place. As we trace the trigger, we need to ask ourselves, "When is the first time I remember feeling this way?" As you trace the trigger back to the root, it will help you identify what is causing the negative behaviors (bad fruit). The feelings that are felt at the time of a trigger are generated and supported by a lie that you believed about yourself the first time you experienced the painful situation. We talked about lies and strongholds in the previous section. If you have a hard time recognizing lies that you are believing, start with the trigger and feelings to help give you clues to recognize the lies.

Our soul remembers the pain of our past very well. Our soul is made up of three parts: the mind, the will, and the emotions. The mind produces our thoughts, the will is what helps us make decisions according to our thoughts, and the emotions are what make up our feelings. When our past triggers the pain, a chain of reactions occurs before we have time to think about it. We first feel the pain in our emotions, then we decide to react to cope with the pain (structure or a coping mechanism). Lastly, we reinforce the mind by believing the distorted reality of the situation. The emotion or feelings felt at the time of the trigger are reminders of the first time you felt the pain of that particular event. When a trigger is set off, it will cause you to respond with an overreaction. Generally, these responses to the trigger and the lies we believe cause the bad fruit of our behavior. As an adult, it's like you are looking at the situation through a magnifying glass at the time of a triggered painful situation. Everything you perceive about the situation seems much more significant and worse than it really is. You will tend to overreact to the situation.

Let me give you an example of what this looked like in my life before I gained healing. As a child, no matter how good of a job I did at cleaning the house or how well I did in school, I didn't get commended for a job well done. This was evidence of a lack of appreciation in childhood. As a mother and wife, I cooked a good meal or worked extra hard to clean the house. Someone complains about the food or makes a mess of my hard work in the house. My pain from an unmet need of appreciation in childhood is triggered. I explode with anger and overreact with yelling and throwing a fit, followed by storming off and isolating myself in my bedroom for the rest of the night.

In response to pain being triggered, we build another layer of hardness around our heart in attempt to protect ourselves against feeling the pain again. This second layer of protection keeps us deeper into a personal prison. It makes it much harder for us to have meaningful relationships with people and God. God may be sending people into your life to help bring healing and happiness, but you can't see the people because you are so locked up in your personal prison. He is sending them as a source of goodness, but you see them as a threat instead. This second layer of the protection wall also further block the ability to recognize God's voice and His attempts to love us.

Coping Mechanisms

As we experience emotional pain, we build coping behavioral patterns to help us deal with it. Coping mechanisms allow us to feel safe for a time, but they hinder us in the long term. They cover up the pain instead of dealing with it. Coping mechanisms keep us trapped in cycles and keep us stuck. Performance (people-pleasing), control, people addiction (codependency), overthinking, and isolation are all examples of coping mechanisms. Other examples are addictions (shopping, smoking, drinking, chemical substances, eating), running from problems, stuffing your pain, passivity, and workaholism.

Picture the coping mechanisms as the cement holding the wall up around your heart. These behavioral patterns make you feel safe, but they cover up the root of the problems that you're actually dealing with. As you cover up the root issues, you never deal with them. Your heart becomes more hardened, blocking your freedom. Each passing day you work your way deeper into survival mode versus stepping out into thriving mode (the fullness of life God intended you to live).

As I left home and started my own life, I thought all my problems from an abusive upbringing were gone. Oh boy, was I wrong. In college, I struggled with depression and low self-esteem. Due to the abuse and lack of nurturing, I believed I had to work harder than anybody else to be good enough, and I needed to be the best at everything so I would be liked and accepted. These beliefs caused me to be a perfectionist and made me work harder to convince people I had value. This left me exhausted all the time because I was continually trying to prove myself to everyone. I could never rest. I had to work harder and harder. I felt invisible, and told myself that if I worked hard enough, maybe someone would notice me and think I was somebody special. As I worked so hard to be accepted by others, I had little left to give to my family. It was exhausting.

On top of working and striving, if I couldn't do something perfectly then I wouldn't even start it. This left me with many ideas in my head and but little to show for it. Even though I didn't see the value in my own dreams and goals, I worked hard to help others achieve theirs. I struggled greatly with performance orientation, trying to show my worth to others.

Entering into marriage, I thought being married would solve my problems and give me the fulfillment I needed in areas where I felt empty. It didn't take long before I realized it was the opposite. Marriage triggered everything that could be triggered. I dealt with a lot of anger, yelling, and isolation. Getting married allowed me to feel safe enough to open my heart more than I had since childhood, so my husband had access to trigger deeper areas of pain than anyone else could. If my husband said anything to me in the slightest tone or used words that made me feel like he wasn't happy with me, I'd either lash out at him or not talk to him for the rest of the night. As I snapped at him, I triggered his areas of buried pain. It started a cycle of arguing, going back and forth, each of us continually triggering past hurt from our childhood.

In motherhood, I recognized bad fruit continuing in my parenting. I promised myself that I wouldn't do the same things my mother and father did, but found myself doing just that. As the pain was triggered in parenting, either from perceived rejection from my toddler or disrespect from my teenager, I resorted to yelling, control, and isolation to deal with it. As I responded out of these coping mechanisms, my children were affected negatively, perpetuating the generational cycle of dysfunction. My triggered behaviors were the same weapons the enemy used to cause wounds and plant lies in my children. The enemy used my bad fruit and my husband's bad fruit to inflict the same poison onto our children. We didn't have the nutrients of love in the soil of our hearts, which caused a void of love to be fed into their hearts as we repeatedly responded to them out of our triggers.

Abandonment

As a little girl, I longed to have that father-daughter relationship. Not growing up with a father was devastating in so many ways. Even as I grew into adulthood, I still longed for that relationship. My expectations came crashing down as my father could never give me the attention or connection I so craved. He was not capable. I tried to fill this need with other father figures in my life who always let me down as well. No other person could ever fill that empty place in my heart.

Imagine your heart like a puzzle. Have you ever tried to make a similar puzzle piece fit where it didn't belong? The wrong puzzle piece might go into the spaces, but you can tell that it doesn't quite work because all the edges don't come together to make a smooth, flowing picture. Your biological parents are kind of like the puzzle pieces that only fit the exact shapes in your heart. The only other piece to the puzzle that can fit perfectly is Jesus. As I started dealing with my abandonment and rejection issues, I found that I was only able to fill those spaces with God's love. The more I filled my life with Him, the more whole my heart became. The love of God can fill all the areas in the puzzle of your heart. So many of us know the pain of having a parent leave the home, either physically or emotionally. Think about that for a moment. That's huge. God intended the parents to be the foundation for your success, and that's exactly what the enemy attacks most. God designed the father to awaken a child's identity and purpose in life. Still, if the father is not there, the child becomes an adult that wanders in life aimlessly, confused about their identity.

As a child, we look to our parents for that reassurance that we are someone special. Suppose your parent's approval and affirming words were not present in childhood. In that case, your heart is open for the enemy to plant lies or seeds of rejection. Not having someone significant to recognize your value causes you to question if you have any value to offer the world. As the enemy makes you question your worth, he wreaks havoc in your mind, will, and emotions trying to stop you from ever stepping into the purpose God called you to. These lies from the enemy keep us stuck.

Picture this: A potter molding a pot. It takes two hands to mold the pot. It takes both hands to mold it because it can become lopsided or even collapse with only one hand. If the potter loses the use of one or both hands, how does the pot get shaped into a masterpiece? This scenario happens when we don't have both parents present to mold us into the masterpiece God designed for us to be. If we didn't have both parents to help mold us, we might become lopsided in some areas of life. Despite this, thankfully our Master Potter and Heavenly Father is more than capable of fixing our imperfections and shaping us into a masterpiece even more beautiful than His original plan. He can use those imperfections as the conduit for His art shining through you and in turn, onto others.

Past Rejection Affects Parenting

How does rejection and abandonment in childhood affect our parenting as an adult? Rejection and abandonment are categories of pain that come with greater levels of wounding in our souls. The lies of rejection can go deeper and be more detrimental than any other pain, making them harder to see past. The rejection we felt in our childhood can cause us to respond to our loved ones through our own lens of rejection. As we react to the lies we believed in childhood from feeling rejected, our actions, attitudes, and tones of voice can cause our spouse and children to feel rejected too. The coping mechanism we use to deal with rejection causes us to close off our hearts and rely on ourselves to avoid feeling rejected again. Without realizing it, we parent out of these coping mechanisms that we established in childhood (self-reliance, self-defense, self-protection, and self-consumption). In dealing with rejection, we tend to try and forget what happened and start blocking the people from our lives who "reject us." As you open your life and heart to a spouse and children, you are sure to be triggered somehow by feelings of rejection. Once again, the typical way people deal with rejection is to push others away if they feel rejected by them. Pushing people away can harm friendships, but the damage is catastrophic when it comes to your family. The walls of self-protection that we put up with our children cause them to feel rejected because of the conditional love we are giving them.

Out of my response to the fear of rejection, I gave my children the message that my love was based on certain conditions. My children had to agree with me, or I felt rejected by them. They had to be compliant, or I felt rejected by them. They had to cater to my needs by giving me hugs and kisses every day, or I felt rejected by them. You see, when I was functioning out of a fear of rejection, it was all about me, when it was supposed to be all about them. As the parent, I should have been taking care of them and helping them feel safe, secure, and loved, but my fear of rejection caused the opposite. Due to my fear of my children rejecting me, I created an environment that was good as long as everyone kept me safe from feeling rejected. If I felt triggered by feelings of rejection, I put my walls up, pushed my children away and isolated myself. As I responded in this way, it left my children feeling rejected, unsafe, and unloved. They felt like they always needed to walk on eggshells around me.

One primary root that caused me to fear rejection was when my grandmother told me that my father was having another daughter with his new wife, and I was no longer going to be daddy's little girl. Even more than the initial abandonment of my father, I felt replaced. I was almost five years old, and I remember feeling devastated, rejected, and tossed aside. For years I denied that this news affected me. I pushed my feelings down, because I was told not to cry and to be a big girl. Without realizing it, this incident left a profound hole in my heart that affected so many decisions and behaviors in my life.

My grandmother's words affected me in all relationships, including my marriage and with my children. This pain caused me to believe that I was replaceable, disposable (like garbage) and not valuable. As soon as my children became more independent and could push me away, I put up walls and pushed them away back. My two-year-old was learning independence, as she should. Because she was busy investigating her surroundings, I perceived this as a rejection. By unknowingly pushing my children away, I deprived them of the love, attention, and affection they so desperately needed. I was too afraid of being "disposed of" or rejected by them. As I started my healing journey, I recognized this and was able to respond differently. The more healed my heart became, the more I was able to show my children the unconditional love and affection they needed.

As my children got older, I tried to control them to keep them close to me. When they started to choose friends, I held tight boundaries about how much time they could spend with friends, who they hung out with, etc. If any relationship or activity appeared to threaten pushing me aside, I would step in to control the situation. To some degree, I responded as a "helicopter mom" if I felt my closeness with my kids would be hindered in any way. I tried to manipulate their thoughts to always agree with me because they might leave me (emotionally or physically) if they disagreed. As my children got old enough to date, I tried to control their relationships more. If they married someone who wasn't like us, the spouse could lead them astray from the family and me. My control issues didn't keep my children close to me. It did the opposite. As they turned seventeen and eighteen, old enough to start acting as adults, they pushed me away. I smothered them and made them feel like they couldn't be individuals. My control kept them trapped and locked up.

I didn't need to know or understand how the news from my grandmother impacted me in order for it to affect my life. When we bury our pain it doesn't go away. It is still there, causing damage to our thoughts and actions. For many years I denied the impact this had on my life, but it remained active underneath the surface. Even though I didn't recognize it was there, I filtered my thoughts, perceptions, feelings, and decisions through that one interaction with my grandmother.

Self Rejection

When we perceive rejection by others it can cause us to start rejecting ourselves. We look in the mirror and hate the person we see, because we start seeing all the things that we think we need to change about ourselves. Self-rejection is one of the most significant barriers that keeps us from being successful in so many areas of life.

Just like the circus trainer puts a chain around a baby elephant's foot to keep him from venturing off, the enemy comes along in childhood to chain us to the lies of our pain. Even though the elephant grows in stature and strength and he has the capability to break free, the elephant stays bound to the chain because he doesn't know he has the power to do so. We grow into adulthood believing that we don't have the value and ability to do great things, even though God created us to do just that.

You must begin to see yourself how God sees you. Rejection is a lie from the pit of hell! When the significant people in your life as a child don't see your worth and value, that doesn't actually mean you are truly less valuable. Those people had wounds in their own hearts blocking the clear vision of all the greatness God placed inside of you. Their wounds created a handicap inside of them that made them blind. But God says that we are entirely accepted and fearfully and wonderfully made. And that's the truth.

Roots of Bitterness and Vows

When someone hurts us, sometimes our response is bitterness and anger mixed with judgment towards that person. Out of anger, our natural response is to blame and judge the person that hurt us. But this response is a trap. Legally, it opens the door for the enemy to access to the part of our lives that mirror the exact thing we judged a parent for in the past. It can keep you bound to a destructive, perpetual cycle that you can't escape from until you recognize it.

Hebrews 12:14-15 ESV says, *"14 Strive for peace with everyone, and for the holiness without which no one will see the Lord. 15 See to it that no one fails to obtain the grace of God; that no "root of bitterness" springs up and causes trouble, and by it many become defiled."*

God warns us about bitterness taking hold in our hearts because the offense will defile us and the people around us. The people that reap the consequences of bitterroot judgments most are those closest to us.

For example, when I was young, my mother was angry and yelled a lot. I judged my mother harshly for yelling and being hostile. The judgment toward my mother stayed hidden in my heart until it became triggered in parenthood. When I became a parent, I started yelling and acting hostile at my children-the very thing I promised myself I would never do. I judged my mother as a child. It caused that same thing to come back to me later in life. For years, my children were negatively affected by my anger and yelling. My judgment toward my mother was a sin. I pridefully considered myself better than her and took God's place as the judge. I also held unforgiveness against her. The judgment I placed on my mother (a parent), resulted in consequences that had greater holds on my life because they coupled with the sin of dishonoring my parent. As I began healing, I recognized the judgment that I had made, I repented and asked God to forgive me. As soon as I did this, the enemy no longer had an open door to my life in that area to cause the cycle to continue. I was able to gain control over my behavior, and the persistent yelling stopped.

Have you judged a parent or someone significant for something that they did to hurt you?

A judgment causes a snare in your soul and traps you in a cycle. The judgment comes back onto you, almost like a boomerang. Matthew 7:1-2 NLT says, *"Do not judge others, and you will not be judged. 2 For you will be treated as you treat others. The standard you use in judging is the standard by which you will be judged."*

Are you doing things in your life that you once judged your parents for? Do you see cycles in your life that remind you of what you disliked about a parent?

Suppose you see a repetitive cycle happening in your life, and it resembles something that you did not like in a parent's behavior. In that case, you are likely reaping consequences from a judgment and vow that you made.

To break free from the effects of a judgment made, you need to recognize the judgment as sin, be sincerely sorry for the sinful response in judgment, ask for forgiveness, and repent for the judgment.

Here is a prayer to break judgments:

> Dear Heavenly Father,
>
> Out of my pain, I confess that I had a bitter-root judgement toward _____ for _____.
>
> I choose to forgive _____ for _____.
>
> Lord please forgive me for judging _____. I repent for the judgment I have made and I renounce and come out of agreement with this judgment. I place this judgment at the foot of the cross.
>
> Lord I release _____ to you. I also release any pain and loss to you.
>
> Please remove any anger or unforgiveness from my heart. Cleanse my heart of all anger and bitterness. Forgive me for taking Your place as Judge.
>
> As I repent, bring an end to the curse and restore Your blessing. Lord, bring evidence in my life that these judgments are no longer active.
>
> In Jesus Name,
> Amen.

Vows

Judgements and vows generally go hand in hand. Vows are promises you made to yourself as you felt hurt and you judged the behavior of the person that hurt you. The promise you made to yourself could be something you thought in your head, believed in your heart, or said out loud. It would sound something like this: "I will never be angry and yell at my child like my mother (or father)." The key phrase here is "I will never…" Proverbs 20:24-25 NIV says, "A person's steps are directed by the Lord. How then can anyone understand their own way? 25 It is a trap to dedicate something rashly and only later to consider one's vows."

When the vow is set into motion, you can spend your whole life working to keep the promise that you made to yourself, and in the meantime reap destructive cycles as a result. In order to be set free from the reaping of the vow, you need to renounce and come out of agreement with it, just like you did with the judgment.

Pray this prayer to break the vows:

> Lord, I confess that I vowed:
>
> I would never _____ like my mother/father.
>
> I come out of agreement with and renounce this vow in the name of Jesus.
> Amen

Iniquity

Not all the things we struggle with come from being directly hurt by someone. Some struggles come down the family bloodline. This type of bondage is called generational curse or iniquity. Iniquity means a bending in one's character towards a sinful nature passed down from previous generations. Just like certain diseases are handed down through your family bloodline, you can have spiritual weaknesses also handed down. Iniquity can be things like lying, sexual addiction, gambling, passivity, anger, etc. The way it works is that we will have a drawing toward a particular sinful behavior. This drawing or leaning towards a sinful behavior causes a temptation for that sin to be stronger.

The Bible says that the iniquities of our fathers can be handed down to the 3rd and 4th generations. Exodus 20:5 NLT says, *"I, the Lord your God, am a jealous God who will not tolerate your affection for any other gods. I lay the sins of the parents upon their children; the entire families affected—even children in the third and fourth generations of those who reject me."* This particular scripture was referring to the sin of worshiping other gods. Still, when it comes to the law of iniquity, it can be any particular sin.

Many times, we may not know that our bad fruit (behavior) comes from a generational cycle. It can be behavior that we look at as "normal" or accepted but can damage our marriage and children. It can also separate our family from God. Isaiah 59:2 NIV says, *"But your iniquities have separated you from your God; your sins have hidden his face from you, so that he will not hear."*

As we recognize that we have repetitive bad fruit or sinful behaviors, we need to evaluate and see if this is something that our parents and grandparents dealt with. Suppose we find that there has been a generational pattern of this behavior. In that case, we need to recognize it, ask for forgiveness (for previous generations as well as ourselves), repent (turn away from it), and resist this behavior. The more we resist the temptations, the stronger the proper response will be, and the less the hold of iniquity will have.

Be Transformed

As children of God we are expected to be transformed in our souls to produce good fruit, the fruits of the Spirit. Galatians 5:22-23 NLT says, *"But the Holy Spirit produces this kind of fruit in our lives: Love, joy, peace, patience, kindness, goodness, faithfulness, gentleness, and self-control. There is no law against these things."*

In John 15:5-8 NLT, Jesus talks about being "in Him" and producing much fruit. Jesus says this: *"Yes, I am the vine; you are the branches. Those who remain in me, and I in them, will produce much fruit. For apart from me you can do nothing. Anyone who does not remain in me is thrown away like a useless branch and withers. Such branches are gathered into a pile to be burned. But if you remain in me and my words remain in you, you may ask for anything you want, and it will be granted! When you produce much fruit, you are my true disciples. This brings great glory to my Father."*

When we remain in Him and His word (the Bible), He remains in us. He says if our branches do not produce good fruit, they will be cut off.

Actions Speak Louder than Words

As we respond to our kids out of triggered pain, ungodly behaviors, and personal wounds, they are being wounded themselves. And we perpetuate a generational pattern. Until we recognize it and fix it the generational patterns will continue. To try and teach our kids the right way, the words we speak will not get through the noise of our wounds. We can go to church and be a good Christian parent, but it all comes out tainted as we try to pour out love on our children. We learn how to cope in life by watching the people around us. It's tough to break free from patterns that are ingrained in us from childhood. The coping mechanisms we put in place to help us deal with the dysfunction become deeply entrenched. Even though we are saved and going to church, we need to allow God to renew our soul to parent the way He wants us to.

Our kids do what we do and not what we say. I correct my kids but then realize that they mirror what they see my husband or myself doing. Many times, I can trace my children's behavior to something that we are doing.

Luke 6: 39-40 NLT says, *"Then Jesus gave the following illustration: What good is it for one blind person to lead another? The first one will fall into a ditch and pull the other down also. A student is not greater than the teacher. But the student who works hard will become like the teacher."*

In this passage, Jesus explains to his disciples that their spiritual condition limits the extent to which they can help others. Jesus refers to it as being spiritually blind. We cannot teach what we do not know. We can't lead someone to a level higher than we have attained.

Will you choose, as a parent, to grab ahold of God and the tools He sets before you to gain healing? Are you going to choose a better life for yourself and your children? Will you accept personal responsibility to grow and gain knowledge of Him so that you can be a better teacher to your children?

When you gain healing, you will love and teach your children with a purer representation of Jesus. As healing takes place, you will be able to become the parent God calls you to be. As a result, your children will be more confident in their identities, know their purposes, and have successful lives.

SECTION 2

GAINING POWER
OVER YOUR PAST

CHAPTER 5

GAIN POWER OVER YOUR PAST

Many resources can teach you how to be a good parent and how to discipline your children appropriately, but until we deal with the root of the problem, your parenting will still be muddled with the rotten fruit of past pain. These principles are foundational to becoming the parent God called you to be. If we continually respond to our children out of our triggered pain, we won't give them the kind of love they need. Our children subsequently grow up deprived of love, and the destructive cycle continues for yet another generation. We must gain healing so that our actions will speak louder than our words. As parents, our most important assignment is to seek God, gain healing, and break dysfunctional patterns to be Christ's example for our children. We are to be filled with His love so that we can pour that same unconditional love into them. Parents set the tone for the whole family. As we gain healing, the love we pour out onto our children will be purer and represent God's love.

We have talked about the things that keep us stuck in life as individuals and as parents. Now we will learn how to move past those things and step into the life that God intended us to have all along.

I am going to teach you five steps to gain POWER over the pain of your past. The power flows from God but is ignited by your decision to embrace the journey. Proverbs 3:16 in the Amplified Bible says, *"May He grant you out of the riches of His glory, to be strengthened and spiritually energized with POWER through His Spirit in your inner self, indwelling your innermost being and personality."*

To achieve victory over your past, you must be determined and decide to work with God, allowing Him to heal your heart. God will do His part in the process, but you have to do your part. As you apply these principles, I believe you will see victory.

"P" is for Pinpoint the Problem

The first step on the road to healing is to pinpoint the problem. Whether it's anger, yelling, insecurity, control, or other issues, you need to recognize them. What is it that you are dealing with that needs to change? In naming your problem, you recognize fruit or behavioral patterns that continue to present themselves. After identifying the negative behavior, we will then trace it back to the first time you remember feeling or behaving that way.

Think back to chapter three and emotional needs. Did you identify with some of the unmet needs in your childhood? Did you recognize some symptoms of those needs not being met in your life? Can you relate to the characteristics of a hardened heart? Do you have bad fruit or issues that come up in parenting?

As you look back over chapter three and the list of emotional needs, identify which areas you had deficits in. This can be a starting point. Those deficits are what produces triggers and negative emotions and behaviors in your life.

When I got married and started having kids, it was then that I realized I had some things about myself that needed to change. As I opened my heart to my children and husband, all the pain from my childhood was triggered. I noticed myself becoming the person I didn't want to be; yelling at my kids, detached, unable to nurture, cold, unloving, depressed, uptight, and controlling. I knew something needed to change.

On my road to emotional healing, there have been ups and downs, roadblocks, speed-bumps, and breakthroughs. I refused to give up on the process of becoming free from emotional bondage. I desired to be a loving mom. I remember how miserable I was before I began this journey. The first time I had a glimpse of hope for a better life was when I listened to a cassette tape series by Joyce Meyer.

My girls were about five, three, and two years old. We rode around in my beat-up station wagon, listening to these tapes. I remember Joyce Meyers saying on these cassette tapes that I could choose to enjoy my children, enjoy my daily responsibilities, and enjoy my everyday life. It never occurred to me that I could choose to enjoy my life. I didn't realize that to have lasting joy, though, I also needed to get to the root of some issues. The first choice that I needed to make was to recognize what needed to change and pursue the path that would bring about the change.

Fast forward ten years, I had been through many emotional healing classes and programs. I thought the level of healing I had gained was as good as it was going to get. After learning about the principles at a Healing the Heart retreat, I recognized that I was still dealing with attitudes, feelings, and symptoms, which revealed that I still needed more healing. Sometimes healing from the most painful issues requires us to lean on God most so that He can reveal those deeper issues to us. These are usually the things we pushed down the hardest, within the depths of our soul. I prayed for God to show me where the root of my insecurity, poor self-image, and feelings of rejection was still coming from. I had healed slightly in these areas, but I could see some symptoms still lingering.

God answered my prayers once again. I shared with you in the last chapter about the situation with my Dad and being replaced as "Daddy's little girl." God allowed me to experience a similar situation that gently reminded me of this moment. All of the feelings of being replaced and pushed aside came rushing back. The pain I endured at just four years old, I buried and dismissed throughout my entire life. I pushed the memory away and wouldn't allow myself to feel the magnitude of this reality. As God answered my prayers, showing me the source of rejection and insecurity, I recognized the impact that this situation had on my life. The pain influenced nearly every decision and action I made. Even though I pushed it aside and ignored the pain, that didn't stop its repercussions. I believed that I was disposable, not valuable, and not good enough. This belief about myself caused me to shrink back and get stuck in a self-defeating mentality my entire life. It held me back from truly stepping into my purpose and calling because I couldn't believe I had worth and value. I felt a level of rejection all my life with anyone I interacted with. Sometimes this step (pinpointing the problem) is easier said than done. So I want you to focus on the negative behaviors or triggers you experience regularly. As you recognize those in your life, trace them back to a painful event that happened in childhood. Make the connections, and we will discuss further what to do with the connections you made.

For me, it was hard to remember things that happened when I was a kid. I blocked out a lot of childhood memories because they were so traumatic. Sometimes we have behaviors that become part of who we are and our identity. Those behaviors are almost like a reflex; they happen without thinking about them. This can make it hard to recognize the behaviors as an abnormal response. It's essential to be in prayer and continually ask the Holy Spirit to help you see your hidden pain. As I mentioned earlier, I had to pray for help to recognize where my deep-rooted, lingering symptoms came from in childhood.

Here are the steps to take to help you pinpoint your problems:
- Recognize reoccurring negative behaviors.
- Recognize symptoms of unmet emotional needs.
- Recognize your negative feelings when they surface.
- Remember the first time you felt that way.
- Trace your symptoms and bad fruit back to an event or unmet need.

O is for Overcome vs. Stay a Victim

As you identify the problem, it is then that you can start the process of overcoming it. Each unmet need and pain of your past needs to be processed individually, one at a time.

At this stage of the healing process, you must realize that you can't wait for the person that hurt you to make things right. For you to gain healing, you must know that it's only God that can heal you. If you wait for the person that hurt you to own up to what they did or to make things right, you may never gain victory. What happened to you in the past might be horrible, but at this point, you aren't a victim anymore. You can make choices to help you move forward in life by working through the past and setting the weight of your past aside.

I used to blame my loneliness and depression on the rejection and abandonment of my father. I longed to have a relationship with him. I thought that if I could have my daddy back, it would solve my issues. Even at age thirty, I waited and hoped for my father to accept and affirm me and give me the attention I needed. The thing is, if parents don't give us what we need by the time we are in the preteen or teen years, chances are they aren't ever going to be able to provide us with what we need emotionally. Before I realized that I would be waiting a lifetime for my father to give me what I needed, I kept wishing and expecting him to be what I needed. As I gained healing, I realized my expectation was a dead end. He absolutely could not emotionally provide me with the love I needed from him, and expecting it from him kept me stuck.

One day I realized that it was my responsibility to process and overcome all that had happened to me in childhood. I was the one that needed to choose to be happy and healthy. I could then pick myself up, connect with Jesus, and start fighting for my freedom, healing, and happiness. We have the choice—new decisions—that can help us overcome the obstacles that have been placed in our path. Through God and the tools He gives us, we can succeed at being loving parents to our children.

Feeling It

As you've gone through the emotional needs section and we've discussed things that have happened in childhood, I'm sure you have feelings surfacing. It can be overwhelming to face things that have been tucked away for a long time. As Denise Boggs says, *"Feelings buried alive don't die."*

To overcome dysfunction, we must begin to face our past by talking about the things that hurt us and feeling the effects again. You may feel like minimizing your feelings, making excuses for them, or even running from them. Give yourself permission to feel the emotions. It is not a sign of weakness but a sign of getting stronger.

The feelings that aren't dealt with will stay inside and affect us in one way or another. They get pushed down and pushed down, and then we add more on top of them. It reminds me of a garbage compactor. We can push it down so tight, but eventually, it hits its limit. The pain will eventually come out sideways or explode as emotions or as sickness within our body.

Face the Pain

What is it that you lost in childhood? Did you lose out on nurturing, approval, encouragement, or any of the other needs you were supposed to have? Did you lose your childhood, having to grow up too soon? Did you lose a parent in the form of abandonment (emotionally or physically absent)? Losses need to be dealt with one at a time.

Choose one thing that you missed out on in childhood or something that happened to you. Identify how you feel. Are you numb, angry, or sad? The next phase of this step is facing the pain. So many people get stuck at this point and don't gain victory. It is at this point that you have to be intentional about pressing into emotional wholeness. Many people use addictions and coping mechanisms to keep themselves from feeling pain and overcoming their issues. The addictions and behavioral structures cause a numbing, and subsequently, the issues aren't dealt with. You must feel the pain to gain freedom.

In Psalms, David gives us an example of how to process pain. David acknowledges that he wants to escape the pain, but instead, he deals with it. To help you face the pain, you need to get the feelings out. You can do this by talking, praying, crying, and writing. As David processed the situation, he also identified who caused the pain. Who do you blame for your pain?

To talk out loud about the pain, you need to find someone that you trust and feel safe with. James 5:16 NKJV says, *"Confess your sins to each other and pray for each other so that you may be healed. The earnest prayer of a righteous person has great power and produces wonderful results."* In sharing your problem with someone, make sure they walk uprightly before God (righteous), are trustworthy, and genuinely have your best interest in mind. You mustn't talk to just anyone and everyone about your problems. The Word says in Proverbs 4:23 NIV, *"Above all else, guard your heart, for everything you do flows from it."*

Here are the steps to take to help you overcome:
- Don't wait for the person who hurt you to make things right.
- Identify who and what hurt you.
- Who did you blame for the pain?
- Give yourself permission to feel.
- Acknowledge your feelings instead of pushing them down or numbing them.
- Push past the pain by talking, praying, and writing.

"W" is for Walk In Forgiveness

Forgiveness may be the last thing you want to talk about and it may even make you feel angry to think about. Many times we think of forgiveness as letting a person off the hook. We want the person who caused us pain to pay for his or her actions. The thing is, Jesus already paid the price for what they did to you. Romans 6:10 says, *"For the death that He died, He died to sin [ending its power and paying the sinner's debt] once and for all; and the life that He lives, He lives to [glorify] God [in unbroken fellowship with Him]. "* Jesus died on the cross for their sins, your sins, and my sins. Forgiveness is not something we do because we feel like it, it is what we do out of obedience to God. If we wait until we feel like forgiving, it will never happen. It is one of the most important steps we need to take to gain healing and victory in our lives.

To forgive means to let go of the pain and bitterness that is keeping us in bondage and giving it to Jesus. When you hold onto bitterness against another person, it's not hurting them. It is only hurting yourself. Holding onto the unforgiveness is like drinking poison and expecting the person who hurt you to be affected.

You will know if you still have unforgiveness in your heart if you think about that person and experience the negative emotions rising up inside you (anger, sadness, or other negative feelings). As long as you hold onto unforgiveness, it keeps your soul from healing. Bitterness stirs up and irritates the wound inside of you. Have you ever had a cut or a bruise that you kept re-injuring? That's kind of what happens when you rehash the pain a person caused you. The bad feelings or negative emotions brought on by unforgiveness are like salt in a wound. Salt makes your wound hurt more. Placing the pain at the foot of the cross will give you freedom and allow you to heal. Research has also shown that harboring bitterness and anger causes sickness and disease inside of our bodies.

Besides physical side effects, bitterness also separates us from God and His blessings. If we do not forgive those that have hurt us, the Bible says that God will not forgive us.

Matthew 6:14-15 KJV says, *"For if you forgive men when they sin against you, your heavenly Father will also forgive you. But if you refuse to forgive others, your Father will not forgive your sins."*

Definition: Forgive—1) Stop feeling angry or resentful toward (someone) for an offense, flaw, or mistake. 2) Cancel (a debt). (Oxford Advanced Learner's Dictionary)

Here is a prayer that you can pray:

Lord,

Your Word says we are to forgive those that have hurt us. Father, I choose to forgive _____(name of person) for _____(what they did). Lord, help me to release them fully from all debts of these hurts. Help me to be free from any bitterness and harsh feeling against this person.

*You can even go a step further in your forgiveness and ask God to bless the person that hurt you. The Bible says to bless those that curse you.

In Jesus name,

Amen

Sometimes the person you may have to forgive is yourself. Forgiving yourself is just as important as forgiving others. 1 John 1:9 NLT says, *"But if we confess our sins to him, he is faithful and just to forgive us our sins and to cleanse us from all wickedness."* As you forgive yourself, you release yourself from the debt, shame, and guilt of a situation. Sometimes you also need to forgive God, if you blamed Him for your pain.

Losing My Father

Even though my relationship with Dad was disappointing, there was a time that I still kept in contact with him sporadically. One night I called him to give him the news that we were expecting another baby. My hopes were that he would be excited and celebrate the idea of having another grandchild, but that wasn't the case. Dad reacted like I had done something very wrong. He started scolding me, and I could hear the disappointment in his voice yet another time. He explained that I had better things to do with my life than have another child. The realization hit me like a ton of bricks. This was the same reaction my mother got when she announced to him her pregnancy with my brother and me. He had not planned for or desired to have children. To him, children were a disappointment and a burden.

A pattern of hurt and disappointment came up every time we talked. I couldn't handle getting hurt anymore. I did what I knew to do. I cut my dad off and wouldn't speak with him anymore. I thought that if I could isolate myself from him, the pain and disappointment would go away and be easier to deal with. Absence makes the heart grow fonder, they say. My bitterness towards Dad grew and grew as the years passed. He needed to apologize for the hurtful things he said and make everything ok again, so I thought. The more years passed, the more the bitterness grew, and the more I resisted forgiving him. It was his fault that my heart hurt so bad, so he needed to be the one to make it right. Then I would forgive him.

Seven years later, Dad called me and left a message on my answering machine. My heart leapt as I heard his voice on the answering machine. Did he miss me? Maybe he was calling to make things right, and we could finally have a good relationship. The disappointment came in once again. He only called to see if my little brother was still alive after his recent car accident. I never returned his call, thinking maybe he would finally learn his lesson if I didn't call him back. I was hurt and I wanted him to hurt as well.

Fast forward to eight months later. My sister sent me a private message on social media. Pam proceeded to tell me that our father was diagnosed with cancer. Her message went on to say that Dad may not have long to live.

The previous seven years flashed before my eyes. All the guilt flooded in from refusing to return Dad's call eight months prior. Pam said that Dad couldn't talk on the phone because he had lung cancer and didn't have enough breath to speak. There was so much that was unsaid between the two of us. The agony that I felt in the pit of my stomach was unbearable. Why did I let things go as I did? I didn't know if I would ever be able to talk to him again.

After much pleading, I persuaded my sister to let me talk to him for a minute. I could only tell him that I loved him and that I planned to see him soon. I had so much more that I wanted to say.

Over the next two days, he seemed to be getting better, so we started planning a family trip to see him. However, the next day, my sister called and told me to catch the next flight to Tennessee because Dad wouldn't make it another 24 hours. He had taken a sharp turn for the worse. Dad had signed a "Do Not Resuscitate" contract the day before, and his lungs had collapsed again.

I booked the next available flight. I had so much I wanted to tell my dad. I wanted to say to him that I loved him, that I forgave him, and that I was sorry for letting our disagreements get in the way of our relationship. I wanted to make amends for everything that I had ever held against him. We landed in Nashville, which is an hour north of my dad's place. We jumped into our rental car and drove extremely fast, knowing that his life was slipping away. As we drove, my sister would ask me, "Where are you now?" A few miles later, she would repeat, "Where are you now?"

Dad was slipping away faster than we could drive. We pulled into the driveway, and my brother and I jumped out of the car. We ran as fast as we could into the house. Dad had passed two minutes before we stepped in the door.

He was trying to hold on for us, but he just wasn't able to. I couldn't believe my dad was gone. I would never be able to talk to him again. There were so many unresolved issues between us.

As I held onto the bitterness all those years, it tormented me and hurt me more than it did him. I was expecting Dad to give me a resolution that he was incapable of giving me. The expectancy that I had of my father kept my heart from healing and having a better life. Letting go of those unobtainable expectations would have given us a chance to connect at least on some level. Unforgiveness stole my joy, fullness of life, and God's blessings.

Hindrances to Forgiveness

My brother took our dad's death hard. Before this, my brother was drinking and doing drugs occasionally, but his drug use spiraled out of control after our dad died. My brother hadn't talked to our dad in over ten years. He also had so many things he wanted to tell him. I never saw my brother cry as hard as he did after discovering that our dad had already passed. We were both hysterical.

Some months following our dad's death, my brother and his wife separated. My brother's drug use escalated, and he began using harder drugs. He withdrew from the family and me. His personality changed so dramatically that I felt I didn't even know him anymore. My brother numbed his pain with any chemical substance he could find.

We took a trip to see him about a year and a half later. He'd lost so much weight that my kids didn't recognize their uncle. When I saw him, I ran to him, crying and begging him to stop the drugs as he looked like he was at death's door. He was nothing but skin and bones. Soon after that, he went to jail, which benefited him temporarily, but he returned to the typical way of life after being released.

The difference between how my brother and I dealt with our father's death was that I ran to God, and he ran to drugs. His drug use helped cover up and numb the pain for a moment, but God takes our pain and heals it forever.

Maybe your coping mechanism isn't a substance. My numbing agent was performance orientation and people-pleasing. When I felt I needed to fix the pain of not being accepted, I would work for someone to give me a drop of acceptance or attention.

To be able to forgive, we need to face the feelings and the loss in order to deal with them. If we numb the pain, we continue the cycle of defeat. When we look to addictions or coping mechanisms rather than looking to God for comfort and healing, we perpetuate the pain. Staying numbed, we block God's healing power. Part of the forgiving process is facing the pain in life and what we lost out on. When you lean on coping mechanisms and numbing agents, you may survive the pain day by day, but instead, God wants us to thrive and overcome it.

Sometimes You Need to Forgive Yourself

I missed out on the opportunity to have any relationship with my Dad all those years, even if it was limited. For a year or two, I beat myself up for the choices I made to block my dad out of my life. I lived with so much regret. I would rehearse all the events leading up to his death over and over again. If I had done things differently, maybe dealing with his death wouldn't hurt so bad. I was so mad at myself. I had to forgive myself for the decisions I had made in my relationship with my dad. I had to let myself off the hook and release everything to God.

Do you need to forgive yourself for something? Do you find yourself feeling bad about decisions you made or something you did? Forgiveness will set you free, even if it's towards yourself. Do you still blame yourself for the way your life has turned out?

I still miss my dad and wish I could talk to him. However, I don't have unbearable pain anymore. God healed me as I faced the loss and forgave myself. My younger brother still numbs and copes with his pain, loss, and unforgiveness with drug use.

To gain healing, you need to forgive whomever you blame for the pain in your life, and sometimes that person may be you. It's vital to go past the sadness and anger and then into forgiveness so that you can release the pain.

As you forgive, you may need to walk through forgiveness on multiple levels before you can completely release the bitterness. Pray for the Lord to help you forgive. You'll feel the weight of bitterness lift and release as you choose to continue giving it to God. You will know that complete forgiveness has been achieved when you think of that person, and the bitterness does not rise within you and even have compassion for the person.

Foregiveness Prayer

Heavenly Father,

Please help me to forgive _____ for
_____. I choose to forgive
_____and accept Your blood as payment in full.

Lord, I choose to release _____
from the prison in my heart.

Cleanse my heart of all bitterness and resentment
towards _____. Wash me clean, Lord.
Help me to recognize when forgiveness is complete.

In Jesus' Name,
Amen

Steps to take to walk in forgiveness:
- Push past anger and sadness.
- Face the pain.
- Recognize who you blame for your pain.
- Forgive the person that hurt you (until the bitterness is gone).
- Forgive yourself.
- Forgive God.

"E" is for Embrace New Thinking

As I gained healing, I realized that the people who caused me pain were not my enemies. They were just hurt people who couldn't take care of me the way I needed to be taken care of. Gaining this realization has helped me release and forgive my mother, father, and others for what happened to me during my childhood.

Identifying the cause of the negative parental behaviors and the lack of my emotional needs met as a child, has helped me unravel the lies that I believed when they happened. The bad fruit that's produced in our lives is a direct result of the lies we believe. Our spirit is renewed when we get saved, but our soul (mind, will, and emotions) are not. So especially as we go through hard times as a child, we need to go through the process of renewing our minds.

In Romans 12:2 NLT it says, *"2 Do not conform to the pattern of this world, but be transformed by the renewing of your mind. Then you will be able to test and approve what God's will is—his good, pleasing, and perfect will. "*

As we transform and renew our thinking with the Word of God, we will see changes in the way we respond to things. We will begin to change into the person God intended us to be, which will help us become better parents.

So you can visualize this process better, imagine my tomato plant we talked about earlier on. The fruit on the plant will represent fruit in our lives. In the first step of the process, we identified some bad fruit. As you see the bad fruit in your life, it is essential to know why the fruit is bad. Now, I want you to imagine the soil in the pot. When the soil is deficient in the nutrients of love and the emotional needs of your childhood, your fruit will not be healthy. Also imagine your thoughts, coping mechanisms, and behavioral structures that are like the support structure for the plant, which may hold the plant upright for a while but eventually the plant gets droopy by all the weight of the bad fruit. The pot also contains weeds and toxins in the form of lies as deficient soil is the perfect environment for the lies to grow. You need to identify what is causing the fruit in your life to be undesirable. What nutrients of love were you missing? What lies are causing weeds to choke out the right kind of fruit in life and parenting? It's important to identify the lies you believed about yourself, your value, or your abilities as the unmet needs or bad events occurred in childhood. The wounds that come from unmet needs and the pain that occurs are what the enemy used to cause you to form a stronghold in your soul. The stronghold in your soul contributed to the wall around your heart, serving as a form of protection. To dismantle this wall, we need to recognize each lie that we are believing.

As you recognize the lies that you believed, you can then start replacing them with the truth of God's Word.

One of the biggest strongholds I had to deal with came during the times of abuse in childhood. As the peacemaker of the family, I was the one that tried to make everyone and everything ok again. Time after time, I would find myself yelling at the abusers to stop hurting my siblings. Screaming at the top of my lungs, I cried and shouted with all passion and everything within me. I cried for them to stop, and they wouldn't stop. The abuse just continued. It was devastating to watch and scream to no avail. As the pattern continued, the enemy whispered in my ear, again and again, "Your words have no power," and "You can't help anyone."

You see, the enemy knew what God created me to do. He knew where to shift my thoughts strategically to keep me from being successful. God's purpose for my life was to use my voice to help people. From the age of thirteen, I had a passion for communications, teaching, and public speaking. I knew that God put that passion in my heart, but I couldn't get past the lie that "my words had no power to help people." I floundered in every attempt to rise to the calling on my life. I felt like I was treading water and not getting anywhere.

As healing in other areas took place, God was then able to show me this particular lie and stone in the wall around my heart. It was one of the most significant strongholds blocking me from stepping into my lifelong purpose. In dealing with the lie, I have been able to see God use my voice in more powerful ways than I could've imagined.

Doing the Work

Knowing the truth does not mean that your emotions will automatically align with the truth. However, as you know the truth, you can come out of agreement with the lies until the truth manifests as your reality. It takes time and requires exercising spiritual muscles that you haven't used before. As you do this over and over, just like lifting weights for your physical muscles, your spiritual muscles get stronger, and it becomes easier and easier to believe and act according to the truth.

Everyday situations can help you uncover the lies you believe. In chapter three, we talked about triggers. Triggers are those feelings that surface when current-day situations are triggered by past pain. Triggers can be feelings of rejection, overreaction, yelling, anger, or projected perception of the current situation. The key is to recognize the feeling when it comes up during your interactions with other people. Most times, the triggers happen with a spouse or your children. The people closest to us tend to trigger us most because we open our hearts more to them than others.

As you recognize negative feelings and reactions to something that was said or done, ask yourself, "When was the first time I remember feeling this way?" And then also ask yourself, "What lie about myself am I believing right now?" Once you answer those questions, you will find what fuels the triggers and the reoccurring pain in your relationships. The solution to stopping the reoccurring pain and subsequent behavior is replacing the lie with the truth in those everyday moments. As you follow this sequence, you will get to the root of the pain and unhealthy behaviors.

Steps to take to embrace new thinking:
- Recognize the negative feelings and triggers.
- Ask yourself, "When was the first time I felt this pain?"
- Next, ask yourself, "What lie about myself am I being challenged with?"
- Come out of agreement with the lie and repent (go the opposite direction in thoughts and actions).
- Replace the lie with the truth found in God's word.

"R" is for Release, Repent, and Resist

As you have forgiven and renewed your mind, it is time to RELEASE. Release the person who hurt you from making things right on their end and release any expectations that you have of that person. When you release the person that hurt you from the debt of unmet needs or reconciliation, you can then allow God to fill those empty places in your heart. If you are still holding onto the pain, you are not in a position to receive what God wants to give you. After you become an adult, the only source that can truly fulfill the longings of your soul for attention, affirmation, and acceptance is your Heavenly Father. As you allow God to fill these empty places, you will then be able to pour into your children. As you go through this process, you will fill your children's needs very naturally. The love will flow as God intended it to flow.

Realizing God's Love

Coming to the knowledge and revelation of God's love will bring much healing and release in your heart. Proverbs 10:12 NLT says, "Hatred stirs up quarrels, but love makes up for all offenses."

Knowing and speaking scripture out loud about what God thinks of you helps you to realign your thoughts of who you are. We are God's children, whom he loves and adores.

Deuteronomy 7:6 NLT assures us, *"For you are a holy people, who belong to the LORD your God. Of all the people on earth, the LORD your God has chosen you to be his own special treasure."*

We must accept and receive his love. If it's hard for you to do this, you can pray and ask the Holy Spirit to help you. He wants us to understand how much he loves us.

When we realize how much God loves us and accepts us, we start to realize that all the hurt we've had in our lives can be overcome. God's love begins to penetrate our soul and starts to take the place of all the pain, offense and judgment. In talking about the root of rejection, which is a huge issue for so many people today, we can tap into God's love and see ourselves the way God sees us.

We no longer need the acceptance of others but only of God. For me, it was hard to realize how much God loved me at first. In my head, I knew he loved me, but I didn't believe it in my heart. It wasn't enough to know it in my head; all the abandonment and rejection issues in my heart were screaming louder than my brain's knowledge about God's love.

In Ephesians, Paul talks about understanding God's love through experience, more than just what we know in our intellect. He explains God infuses us with His Holy Spirit and indwelling our INNERMOST BEING AND PERSONALITY. When God infuses us, He influences our personality and how we act and respond to people and things around us. When we are infused with God, He can affect how we parent our children. He changes our responses. Furthermore, when we EXPERIENCE His love and not just have HEAD KNOWLEDGE of His love, He can carry out His purposes in our lives more than we can ask or think.

Ephesians 3:16-20 AMP says, *"16 May He grant you out of the riches of His glory, to be strengthened and spiritually energized with power through His Spirit in your inner self, [indwelling your innermost being and personality], 17 so that Christ may dwell in your hearts through your faith. And may you, having been [deeply] rooted and [securely] grounded in love, 18 be fully capable of comprehending with all the saints (God's people) the width and length and height and depth of His love [fully experiencing that amazing, endless love]; 19 and [that you may come] to know [practically, through personal experience] the love of Christ which far surpasses [mere] knowledge [without experience], that you may be filled up [throughout your being] to all the fullness of God [so that you may have the richest experience of God's presence in your lives, completely filled and flooded with God Himself]. 20 Now to Him who is able to [carry out His purpose and] do superabundantly more than all that we dare ask or think [infinitely beyond our greatest prayers, hopes, or dreams], according to His power that is at work within us."*

Many of us have a hard time comprehending His love's width, height and depth, because we measure His love by the love we received from our parents. This is where it takes the real, tangible experience with God to move past our preconceived ideas of God's character and love.

When you allow His love to flow through your heart, He brings the healing ability to release all of the pain, bitterness, and whatever keeps you stuck. So how do we actually experience God's love? It wasn't until I started spending diligent, quality time with God-praying, reading my Bible, and worshipping Him-that I experienced it. I just started talking to Him and listening for His responses back to me. Reading the Bible was hard for me. I don't know about you, but it was hard to understand when I first started reading my Bible. As I continued to read each day, God began to help me understand it, and the words came alive. The Bible began affecting how I thought, acted, and believed. If you are struggling with reading the bible, ask the Holy Spirit for clarity and understanding. During this time with God, I also found worship songs that spoke to me and expressed my feelings and thoughts back to God. I soaked in God's presence by listening to music and listening for God to speak to me. As I continued to spend time with Him, I began to experience the river of God's love that went deep into my heart. Now, my heart was very empty and lacking from childhood, so it took me a while of diligently spending time in God's presence before I felt any changes. When I started experiencing God's love filling my heart, I began to see changes in how I responded as a parent. I began to feel the healing power of His love affecting all areas of my life.

Personalize Your Prayer

When you pray, speak the Word out loud. Scripture is God's Word, and when you declare God's Word, you activate God's hand to accomplish what He says in His Word. As you pray scripture, your prayers become very powerful. I pray Ephesians 3:16-20 over myself and my family.

My prayer sounds something like this:

> Lord,
>
> Grant me, out of the riches of your glory, to be strengthened and spiritually energized with power through your Spirit in MY inner self, indwelling MY innermost being and personal-

ity, so that you may dwell in MY heart through MY faith. And may I, having been [deeply] rooted and [securely] grounded in love, be fully capable of comprehending with all God's people, the width and length and height and depth of your love, fully experiencing that amazing, endless love. And may I come to know [practically, through personal experience] your love, which far surpasses knowledge [without experience]. May I be filled up [throughout MY being] with all the fullness of you, God, so that I may have the richest experience of your presence in MY life, being completely filled and flooded with you, God. Carry out your purpose in MY life and do superabundantly more than all I dare ask or think [infinitely beyond our greatest prayers, hopes, or dreams], according to Your power that is at work within me.

In Jesus Name,
Amen

As you are able to know God, you can trust Him with your heart. Trust Him with the things that you thought you needed to control. The coping mechanisms and behaviors you once needed in order to feel safe and cope with life, are no longer required. As you release your life into the hands of Jesus, He can rebuild your heart and life. He starts to turn your hardened heart of stone into a heart of flesh, referred to in Ezekiel 36:26. This is where your bad fruit turns into good fruit.

In John 15:1-11 AMP, Jesus says, *"I am the true Vine, and My Father is the vinedresser. 2 Every branch in Me that does not bear fruit, He takes away; and every branch that continues to bear fruit, He [repeatedly] prunes, so that it will bear more fruit [even richer and finer fruit]. 3 You are already clean because of the Word which I have given you [the teachings which I have discussed with you]. 4 Remain in Me, and I [will remain] in you. Just as no branch can bear fruit by itself without remaining in the vine, neither can you [bear fruit, producing evidence of your faith] unless you remain in Me. 5 [b]I am the Vine; you are the branches. The one who remains in Me and I in him bears much fruit, for [otherwise] apart from Me [that is, cut off from vital union with Me] you can do nothing. 6 If anyone does not remain in Me, he is thrown out like a [broken off] branch, and withers and dies; and they gather such branches and throw them into the fire, and they are burned. 7 If you remain in Me and My words remain in you [that is, if we are vitally united and My message lives in your heart], ask whatever you wish and it will be done for you. 8 My Father is glorified and honored by this, when you bear much fruit, and prove yourselves to be My [true] disciples. 9 I have loved you just as the Father has loved Me; remain in My love [and do not doubt My love for you]. 10 If you keep My commandments and obey My teaching, you will remain in My love, just as I have kept My Father's commandments and remain in His love. 11 I have told you these things so that My joy and delight may be in you, and that your joy may be made full and complete and overflowing."*

In summary of this passage, Jesus says that if we stay in Him and Him in us (spending time with Him and reading the Word of God daily), we will produce good fruit. He will get rid of (prune) the bad fruit so that the good fruit will grow.

After I started to understand the releasing part of this process, I began to see significant milestones in my healing journey. As I shared with you, one of my coping mechanisms was performance. I functioned in performance, working to gain acceptance, affirmation, and attention from people.

I worked harder than anyone around me. I had to say yes to everything and everyone, even if God wasn't calling me to it, or I really didn't want to do it. I had to be seen as the most "valuable" employee, church member, friend, wife, and mom. If I could do enough "good works" for people, they would surely see that I was valuable and accept and love me. That was the problem! I wasn't working to please God but to please people. I worked so hard to earn people's approval that I finally reached a point of burnout. No matter how much good works I did, I couldn't get enough love, acceptance, affirmation, or attention from people to fill those deficits in my heart. I still felt empty all the time. I still felt invisible and unvalued. The only thing that was able to fill me was God's love. I had to feel His love.

As I recognized that performance was my coping mechanism and the way I dealt with the emptiness of childhood, I resisted and repented of it. Each time I was tempted to say "yes" to someone, I had to check my heart and see if I was trying to please people or God. Was I trying to gain love and acceptance from the person that asked me to do this job? Am I working on this project to keep myself from rejection? If I answered yes to these questions, then I resisted my urge to do whatever the job was. As I functioned in this coping mechanism, I blocked God from showing me His love and my value according to Him. Pleasing people took the place of pleasing Him. As I took the step of faith in allowing God to protect me and show me how much He valued me, I was able to see and experience God's love. Every situation when I allowed God to protect and show me He's taking care of me, caused more healing to come into my heart. If we take matters into our own hands and try to fill our own needs and protect ourselves, it keeps God from taking care of us and keeps Him from being able to show his love to us.

Release and Resist Old Ways

As you release things in your life and go through the process of getting rid of destructive patterns, you need to resist the tendency to go back into old ways. The coping mechanisms and old ways of dealing with problems became so ingrained in how we handled things in our past that they can come back on a subconscious level. As we recognize when old behavioral patterns, thinking patterns and responses creep back in, we must guard against the behaviors and resist them. As you resist the bad fruit and bad thinking, God will show you His provisions and His hand moving you towards a better way of life. You need to resist old behaviors and thoughts, turn and acknowledge God, and decide to agree with God's ways and His truth. The more you resist the sin, the less hold it will have on your life.

Steps to take to release, repent, and resist:
- Release the people that hurt you.
- Release the debt of the ones that hurt you.
- Release the expectation of the ones that let you down.
- Recognize what coping mechanisms take the place of God filling your needs.
- Open your heart and let God be your source.
- Resist old behaviors.

SECTION 3

PARENTING WITH
NEW PERSPECTIVE

CHAPTER 6

UNDERSTANDING OUR CHILDREN

A s you unravel your past, it's easier to move forward to be the parent God has called you to be. Understanding where the gaps and deficits were in your childhood can create an opportunity for greater awareness and the ability to fill the gaps in the emotional needs of your children. As you go through the following three chapters, focus on learning how to filter your responses through these emotional needs. The more you filter your responses, the more you will allow love to flow the way God intended.

Acceptance

Feeling approved of and accepted is one of the most foundational needs your child has. Whether boy or girl, compliant or strong-willed, athletic or academic, blonde or brunette; your child needs to know you completely accept them for who they are. They begin to feel acceptance, or lack thereof, in utero. If pregnancy begins and the conception of the baby is not joyfully embraced, the baby feels rejection. Acceptance is demonstrating unconditional love to your child. When we love unconditionally, they don't feel like they have to measure up to our expectations.

Definition: Unconditional—not subject to conditions (Oxford Advanced Learner's Dictionary)

As your child feels approval without conditions, they will trust you and feel like they can come to you anytime, with anything, as they get older. As our Heavenly Father gives us unconditional love, so should we do the same for our kids. Our kids are just like us, they are going to mess up and make mistakes, but they need to know we have their backs in every trial and tribulation of life.

Let them Know They are Accepted

There are things you can do to ensure that your child feels accepted. Facial expressions and tone of voice is the first indicator to your child that you accept and love them. As your child grows and starts getting into trouble or pushing your buttons, it is important to know that facial expression and tone of voice will communicate either acceptance or rejection depending on how you react to the situation. It is so important to reassure your child in correcting and disciplining, using reassuring and nurturing words, hugs, and affection. One way you can reassure them is to explain and talk about the behavior. While talking it out, though, be sure to separate the unaccepted behavior from the child (make it clear that the behavior was unacceptable). Example: "Joshua, your behavior was unacceptable today," vs. "Joshua, you were a bad boy." Make sure to show love during times not coinciding with good works, letting them know you accept them just the way they are, and that your love is not dependant on their performance. Lastly, as your child learns to become an individual with his or her own thoughts and ideas, it is essential to give your child room to disagree and still be loved and accepted.

How to show approval and acceptance:

- •For babies and younger children, assure them by smiling at them and talking to them often.

- • Make sure to communicate to your child that they are loved, just the way they are.

- • After correction or discipline, reassure them with love and acceptance (using reassuring words, hugs, and affection).

- • Separate the unaccepted behavior from the child (make it clear that the behavior was unacceptable) Example: "Joshua, your behavior was unacceptable today," versus, "Joshua you were a bad boy."

- • Assure your child that they can have their own opinion. Make sure to show love during times not co-inciding with good works.

- • After a competitive activity, use language like "Did you have fun?" vs "Did you win?"

Warning Signs

There are warning signs that your child will show if they aren't feeling accepted. You may hear your child compete with or compare themselves with their siblings (who did better or more). As with my third-born, they may voice feelings of rejection or not fitting in for no apparent reason. They may say things like, "You love them more than me." A child that is acting shy or withdrawn, excessively crying, hard to console, or always defensive, may be feeling a lack of acceptance.

The Root of Rejection

Suppose a strong sense of acceptance isn't established even from conception. In that case, a root of rejection can form in our child's soul in utero. Rejection is the opposite of acceptance.

My daughter, Arriah, had a deep root of rejection planted while she was in my womb. I became pregnant with Arriah five months after giving birth to my second child, Karrah. The idea of being pregnant so soon after giving birth was overwhelming. Negative thoughts and emotions plagued me. For a couple of weeks after I found out that I was pregnant, I cried. Instead of being happy and feeling blessed with another child, I was miserable. I was rejecting my blessing from God. The baby inside of the womb can feel and sense our emotions. Arriah felt my initial reaction of rejection of her, even as a fetus.

After that initial shock faded, I began to embrace my pregnancy with her. However, it was too late. The seed of rejection was already planted in my daughter's soul. She thought I didn't want her and that she was a mistake. Soon after she was born, I realized she was a miserable baby. As she grew into a toddler, she became increasingly miserable. I thought something was physically wrong with her because she cried constantly. She was rarely happy. I couldn't understand why she cried and cried for no apparent reason.

As a young girl, despite all the attempts to give her extra attention and make her feel loved, she complained, "No one loves me," or she would ask, "Why do you love my sister more than me?" She felt rejected easily and often.

As a teenager, she became depressed, withdrawn, and defensive. She acted differently from her sisters. We could not figure out where we were going wrong with this child. Why did she feel like we didn't love her and didn't want her? She tried to tell us what was bothering her, but it didn't make sense most of the time. Her perception was slanted and twisted by her wound of rejection; I didn't know how to help her feel better. It didn't make sense in the natural situation because it was a spiritual problem. It was a more profound emotional issue than what we could figure out on the surface.

When I started to learn about emotional healing, I realized that we were dealing with the root of rejection. I started praying for the strategy to help her. Also, because she was old enough to have a spiritual understanding of things, I shared with her what had happened when I conceived her. We talked together about ways to get to the root of her feeling this way.

Arriah started to read about the spiritual dynamics of rejection. She began to press into God on her own. Within a short time, she transformed into a different person. I saw her perception and attitude change dramatically. Because God turned the light on in the dark room of Arriah's heart, revealing the lies of rejection, she gained healing. Since that time, Arriah has blossomed into a mighty young woman of God.

Stability

Stability is the need to feel safe and secure (emotionally and physically). It means a home that is free from physical, verbal, and emotional abuse. Your home should be a safe, peaceful sanctuary for everyone to enjoy. As there is love and harmony between mother and father and also with the children, they will feel secure.

Helping Them Feel Secure

To make sure your home feels secure, you must create a home of harmony, free from danger. One way to create peace in the home is to work through personal healing for better relationships with your spouse and others in the household. Another way to establish security in the home is to make sure there are fair household rules with clear and comparable consequences if those rules are broken. Most importantly, it is imperative to teach your children how to trust God. Then, as they grow into adults, they will need to lean on God for their security in all areas of life. If you notice that your child is experiencing excessive fear, worry, nervousness, feeling unsettled, lacking peace, or obsessive-compulsive tendencies, these are signs that they do not feel safe and secure.

Create Stability

Creating stability in your child's life helps her/him feel safe and secure in their environment and in who they are. Stability is created by forming a consistency in the way you do things and in what you expect.

Definition: Stable—Not likely to change or fail; firmly established (Oxford Advanced Learner's Dictionary)

How to create stability in the home:
- Provide a home safe from danger.
- Create a home of harmony. Work through personal healing for better relationships with your spouse and others in the home.
- Establish fair and consistent household rules.
- Establish fair consequences that match the broken rules.
- Teach about faith by involving them in prayer and when God provides the answer.

Establish consistent rules, create a predictable schedule, and have consistent consequences. When children have a clear understanding of what the rules and expectations are, they feel secure. Discipline out of love and not anger or hurtful emotions. Having consistency and schedules doesn't mean that things have to be rigid. We can have spontaneous ideas and events. However, these are the exceptions, not the rule. In general, we should have some sense of the way things are supposed to function in our households.

My older children, who are out on their own, have thanked me for the boundaries we had set when they were younger and even as teenagers. Their teen friends who had no boundaries or rules ran wild and were slow to develop senses of responsibility. They said boundaries gave them a sense of security and helped them grow into responsible adults.

Parents In Harmony

Working towards harmony with your spouse is one of the foundational components of creating security in your home. As parents show stability in their relationship with love and respect towards one another, it makes the children feel stable and secure.

I remember so many times listening to my step-dad and my mother arguing. I would have a knot in my stomach, thinking that my world was going to crumble once again. I remember the insecurities and anxiety that welled up inside of me. But, on the other hand, I remember feeling so happy and secure once my mother and step-father made up and were getting along again.

Now that I'm grown and have kids of my own, I look back at that contrast to remember how I felt as a child. When my husband and I argue about something, the Lord reminds me of how this behavior affected me as a young child. It helps me remember that the parents set the tone for the household. If mom and dad are fighting and living in strife, there will be strife in the children. Parental strife darkens the spiritual atmosphere for the entire family.

Set Family Rules

Each family needs to decide which rules to establish in their household. Look at biblical guidelines for Christian behavior and go from there. There are things that I may not allow in my family, but you may think they are perfectly fine. I believe if you read God's word and yield to His voice, all while asking for wisdom along the way, you will be able to establish a good foundation of rules and boundaries for your children.

As you establish the rules for your family, talk about them, make sure everyone understands them, and have consequences for breaking the rules. There are times when we need to put our foot down, and there are times when we need to extend grace. Deciphering this is all a matter of godly wisdom and discernment.

Consistency is Key

Once we have our rules in place, consistency is the key. Consistency helps establish the family structure.

Definition: Consistency— The achievement of a level of performance that does not vary greatly in quality over time. (Oxford Advanced Learner's Dictionary)

We need to know the desired behavior outcomes we are looking for in our children and stick to our rules no matter how tough it gets. We don't always feel like being consistent. Consistency is hard to have when we are tired or overwhelmed. When we lose our way for a few days in staying consistent, we can realize our children are getting out of hand. It is easy for children to start slipping into past behavioral patterns and bad habits when we lose consistency and stop following through with discipline.

Consistent Consequences

After you establish rules and boundaries, it's time to reinforce them. When rules aren't followed, and boundaries are crossed, there needs to be consequences. Discipline is crucial in molding our children's behavior. There are many ways you can discipline wrong behavior, but the key factor is that it is consistent and fair.

There needs to be a clear-cut plan. If your child breaks a particular rule, then there will be corresponding discipline. The key to building security is to make sure the consequences match the behavior and not overreact to the broken rule. In our house, we use time out, spanking, writing scripture, and grounding.

After discipline takes place, we make time to talk. We sit down with the child and talk about what happened. As we talk about what happened, we brainstorm better ways to handle the situation. We re-explain the rules and boundaries and ask if the child understands why they were disciplined. We hug and love them to reassure them that they are loved.

Imparting and Teaching Faith

I have vivid memories of going through some challenging times when our girls were little. One of those times is when my husband lost his job. My husband and I would call a family meeting, and we would share with our children the basic gist of what was going on. We all prayed and talked about the situations together. We also would turn on music and worship our way through the challenging moments. My girls and I would dance around our home, thanking God that He was answering our prayers. Worship was a great way to lighten the mood of our challenging times, and it would teach our children to praise God amid struggles.

Whenever we go through life's challenges, we include our children. When our children were little, there were some things that we needed to protect them from knowing, but for the most part, we included them in prayers, decision-making, and navigating through life's challenges. On the flip side of that, when we saw God answer our prayers, we celebrated together. As we included our children in life's challenges and celebrating the victories together, they learned how to go to God and His word to deal with things biblically.

As we teach our children to have faith in God, they gain security beyond what we can provide for them as parents. Having faith in God is the ultimate form of security as they learn from experience. As a result, we set them up for a rock-solid foundation as they grow into adults and have to trust God for things apart from us.

Family Traditions

Establishing family traditions is another way of bonding and spending time together. Building memories and the consistency of enjoyable things to look forward to creates another aspect of stability and security. Each year around Christmas time, we went to our local tree farm to cut down our Christmas tree together. We rode the hay wagon, went out into the woods, and found the perfect tree together. Everyone had to agree on the tree before we cut it down. Then we went home to enjoy hot chocolate and cookies while we decorated our tree together. We started this tradition when our girls were little and did it every year. They looked forward to it and were so excited with expectation as the time grew nearer for us to go every year. This tradition and others created a sense of unity and helped us to grow closer as a family.

Our girls, as adults, talk about our family traditions to this day and how the traditions drew our family together and created memorable moments. They have established traditions of their own, with their families, knowing how important it was as they were growing up.

Respect

Respect is a way of regarding each other with value in the home, including your children. This need becomes especially important as a child grows into the preteen and teenager years.

You can help your child feel respected by speaking to them the way you want to be spoken to (tone and words). Protecting your children from embarrassment in front of friends and in public is another way to model respect. In older children, it is necessary to respect your child's privacy and property.

How to model respect:
- Protect your children from embarrassment in front of friends and in public.
- Respect your child's privacy.
- Respect your child's property.
- Speak to your children the way you want to be spoken to (tone and words).

If your child has not felt respected, they will tend to be rebellious and disrespectful to authority figures (parents and teachers) and even peers. They may demand respect by bullying their peers. A child who has struggled with feeling respected may, on the other hand, feel inferior or insecure. A lack of respect will cause an older child to feel like they can't trust you, hide things from you and not come to you with something they are dealing with.

Teaching Respect by Example

One day I had a revelation that changed the way I responded to my children. Just because our children were little people and younger than us didn't make them any less important. I realized we need to treat our children the same way we, as parents, want to be treated.

In Matthew 7:12 NLT Jesus said, *"Do to others whatever you would like them to do to you. This is the essence of all that is thought in the law and the prophets."*

Jesus didn't make an exception. He wasn't telling us to treat others how we want to be treated, except for our children. We need to show respect to our children and each other to understand what respect is.

Children learn by example by doing what we do and not just what we say. We can tell our children all day long how to respect adults and teach them respect, but until we are living it, they won't learn it very well. When we are living out of our dysfunction, we treat our children disrespectfully. Our tone of voice is demeaning, and we treat them with less respect than we would treat an adult or our spouse. I see this all the time in the grocery store. A parent treats their child as if the child doesn't have the same feelings as an adult.

Our children are little people who always need constant correcting and training (guidance). However, we need to discipline in a considerate way and how we would want to be corrected. We need to communicate respect from the time they are babies right on up through their adult years. Like mirrors, they will reflect the respect we show for them back to us and others.

For example, A child is acting out in the store. In the act of disrespect, the parent grabs the child by the arm and starts publicly yanking the child around, with a tone and words that tear that child's tiny heart apart. On the other hand, a respectful parent will protect the child's feelings by pulling the child to the side while calmly explaining why the behavior is inappropriate. It may even be necessary to leave the store and return another day, but the child's self-worth is left intact.

I realized the value of instilling mutual respect as our children reached their teen years. At this point, if a teen doesn't feel like you respect him or her, the teen will start to rebel. Respect is one of the most foundational parts of having a stable, healthy, happy teenager. When our children grow to be teens, they want to feel like a trusted and respected individual. If they don't feel like we trust and respect them, they hide things from us and don't come to us with their problems. When our kids stop coming to us with their problems, it shuts down the line of communication. They start looking for advice other places and from their peers. When you forfeit the right to speak into your teen's life because you failed to respect them, you lose all ability to influence them. Lack of respect is one of the primary causes of division in most families when children hit their teen years.

It Filters Down

One day I was analyzing the interaction between my older children and my younger children. The older children were constantly disrespecting the younger ones. I realized, once again, that they were mirroring the attitudes that we had toward them when they were younger. My girls sounded just like I did when speaking to them as young children. They had adopted the same attitudes with their little brothers. We had taught our children, by our actions, that it was ok to treat someone younger than themselves disrespectfully. If you establish a precedent of disrespect in your family, the home will be a hostile environment.

Watch the Tone

The tone of your voice and the attitude you use with your children makes a huge difference in the way they respond. One day, I was teaching my 12-year-old a new chore: how to vacuum. He really didn't want to do chores at the moment, so he had a resistant attitude from the get-go. In response to his poor attitude and lack of respect, I got an attitude.

I began talking very sternly to him and was snappy and naggy. My goal was to teach him in a way that God would have me teach him, but I soon realized I was not accomplishing that.

I wanted him to learn how to do good work with a good attitude so that he could develop a good work ethic. This particular child consistently gave me a hard time about work ethic. The more I tried to teach him, the more he resisted.

I became so frustrated that I began to pray silently: "Lord help him, Lord help me," over and over. Then I started praying, "Lord, give me wisdom and help me teach him the way you would teach him."

I didn't want to lose my temper, which might create resentment or possibly wound his spirit. God simply told me, "Change your tone." I immediately changed my tone and my attitude. My motive at that moment changed in my heart. Instead of treating him as a rebellious preteen, compassion and love filled my heart. My voice softened, and I spoke to him in love.

It was like a switch flipped in me, and as soon as it did, his attitude changed immediately. He then became much more teachable and tenderhearted. He listened to me and did as I asked. I saw such a huge difference in him and how he responded as soon as I changed my attitude.

We may not feel like acting respectfully towards our children, especially if they are acting out of disrespect, rebellion, or with bad attitudes. This incident proved to me that we have a choice to make. We can pray for God's direction and make a choice to obey God. I had to lead by example. I didn't feel like changing my attitude, but when I did, it shifted the whole dynamics in our relationship for the better.

Looking back at this, I now realize that my tone had changed in this situation because my son triggered my pain from childhood, not having been respected. I felt entitled and demanded he show me respect, even though I wasn't respecting him. My pain and response defiled him and caused him to respond to me in the exact same way.

Our children know if we are acting out of love or acting on our wounds. If we truly have a loving heart when responding to our children, we have a lot better chance of reaching their hearts. I had to adjust my attitude.

1 Corinthians 13:1 NKJV says, *"Though I speak with the tongues of men and of angels, but have not love, I have become sounding brass or clanging cymbal."*

I'm quite certain my 12-year-old heard clanging cymbals when I initially talked to him that day. I wanted him to learn to do a good job for my benefit, not his. My true motive became apparent by how I was treating him. I didn't want to be bothered by his attitude or the time it was taking to teach him how to do a good job. I wanted a clean house, but I wasn't really focused on how this would help him be a loving husband and dependable worker in the future. As soon as I changed my attitude, we connected, and he complied. Instead of creating division, I created a connection. This helped us grow closer in our relationship.

CHAPTER 7

SPENDING TIME TOGETHER

S pending time with your kids is imperative in shaping and training them into the people we and God wants them to become. When our children are young, the time we spend building memories and bonding with them creates a sense of togetherness and stability. Spending time together as a family lets our children know we value them. When our children are young, the time and value we place on our relationships builds credibility as they grow into their preteen and teen years. As teens, they will look to spend time with us and allow us to influence their development.

As a family, we work hard to cultivate closeness in our children and their relationships with each other. In our family, we spend a lot of time together. Family time is a high priority, and we guard that time even as life gets busy.

As parents, we tend to either get busy with "adult things" or we are so tired we tend to fade out in television or technology to relax.

Time with our children goes by so fast. They grow up much quicker than we could imagine. If we aren't careful, we could have that critical time pass us by before we know it. We have a window of time to capture the hearts of our children. Suppose we are too busy doing our own thing. In that case, we could lose the opportunity to connect with our children in a way that will continue to make a difference in their lives.

Give Them Attention

Attention is one of the most crucial needs a child has. As you spend time connecting with them on their level, you will create a bond and strong relationship that will help lay the foundation for years to come. If your child is not getting enough attention, they may be trying to gain attention from other sources like social media, opposite gender, or teachers. They also may be hyperactive, loud, disruptive, rebellious, obsessed with their appearance, competitive with siblings, or talk about themselves excessively. Giving adequate, consistent attention in childhood will produce self-confidence and a strong self-esteem.

Here are some ideas to give your child attention:
- Quality time together (one on one time if you have multiple children)
- Playing games with your child
- Coloring with them
- Listen intently to what they are saying
- Have meaningful conversations with them
- Show you care about what is important to them (all ages).
- Dads, tell your daughter how beautiful she is.
- Moms, tell your son how handsome he is.
- Regular Bible study and prayer time
- For older children, be an active participant in their activities.

Daily Devotions

At bedtime, my husband or I will read some scripture to our children at bedtime, explain it, and teach them how it applies to life. At first, we weren't diligent in doing this. It seemed so hard to find the time. We had to figure out what we were going to read to them and how we would teach them. However, after we made this a daily habit, we saw a big difference in our kids.

On nights that we were running late, we tried to skip the devotion-that did not go over well with our kids. It turns out our kids love having that structured devotion time. We started out reading parts of Proverbs to our children because it has incredibly wise instruction that is easy to teach and understand. It helped us get accustomed to reading regularly, and we could explain the meaning of the scriptures to them.

As we have faithfully continued, we have found different devotionals to help us. If you are reading scripture to your child, you are building a good foundation for life. If you begin a routine of reading and drift off track, get back on track as soon as you can. As you build consistency in their lives of hearing God's word, it will build stability for them.

One-on-One Time

Simple things like taking one child at a time on an errand is time well spent. When we spend one-on-one time with our children, we get to talk with them and know them better. I find that when I spend "alone time" with my kids, they want to tell me everything they can about what they've been doing and thinking. It's in these times that we can learn so much about our kids' hearts, thoughts, and talents. Also, that alone time builds a sense of intimacy with each child. It helps each child know they are special because you have taken time for just them. This is undivided attention.

If We Don't Spend That Time Together

If we don't spend quality time with our children, they may very well end up drifting away from us, God, and the things we've taught them. There are examples in the Bible of fathers who were busy with ministry and doing God's work but didn't pay attention to their kids.

Let's take a look at High Priest Eli in 1 Samuel. Eli had sons, and he was given the job of mentoring Samuel from the age of three. I guess you could say Samuel was a spiritual son to Eli. The scripture says that Eli did a great job mentoring Samuel, but Eli ignored bringing up his boys. His boys had many problems with being self-absorbed, rebellious, and didn't want to follow God.

The people of Israel were upset about the things these boys were doing, and God was upset with how they behaved. Eli talked to his sons, but his sons were older and already set in their rebellious mindsets. His talk did no good. From reading the scriptures, can we conclude that Eli may have been guilty of being preoccupied with his ministry? He tolerated sin in his children and did not take time to pour into them while he was pouring into Samuel and the people of Israel. I have seen families where the parents get busy with work and activities that don't include their kids. The kids stray away from God and the family unit. I've seen children without a strong family bond who create "family" with friends and people that aren't good influences. Sadly, many pastors are so focused on their ministry they neglect their children.

As humans, God created us to need that connection and sense of belonging. If our kids don't feel the sense of belonging from us, as their parents, they will look for other groups of people to belong to. The statistics show that this is the biggest reason a kid will choose to enter a gang relationship. They want and need to belong.

Take Time to Talk

As our girls have grown into adults, we've learned that communicating and talking with our kids is one of the most important things to do when we spend time together. When we sit and talk with our kids, it's a time that we can help them sort things out in their heads and hearts. In talking to our kids, we are helping them establish a sense of identity. When we talk about life's situations, it helps them figure out who they are and who they want to be. We can influence them positively by taking time to talk to them about the Bible, God, and our past experiences. When we genuinely care about what our kids have to say and listen to what they are going through, even our teens will talk with us. Not only will our kids talk to us, but if we build that bond and trust with them, they will appreciate us as a parent and as a close friend.

I've spent so much time talking with my girls about the courting/dating process, friendships, shortcomings in their spiritual lives, how to grow spiritually, and what's right and wrong in certain situations. My boys are quite a bit younger than my girls, so our topics are different, but we also take time to sit and talk with them. Talking with our children while they are young sets the stage for trust and provides the comfort they need to confide in us later.

As we spend time talking with our children and helping them sort through things, it helps them learn communication skills. Communication is so important. It is the foundation of so many facets of life. Our kids will need to communicate with their spouses, their bosses, and the people around them. As we talk with them, we give them guidance and life skills to help them be successful in life. Communicating with our kids helps them learn how to deal with the ups and downs of life, functionally and methodically.

Schedule Family Time

We value family time, and we designate time in our schedules for it. If we don't purpose in our hearts to have family time, it won't happen. There are times we have to say no to other things to make sure we have family time. Family time is simply spending time together as a family. There are so many ways you can spend time together. Family time can be simple and doesn't need to cost money.

Sitting down as a family during mealtime is particularly important. Even if we have chicken strips or hot dogs, we still set the table and eat together. Dinner time gives us the ability to connect and find out what's going on in each of our lives. It's a lot harder to get everyone together as our kids are getting jobs and growing up. Still, we keep the tradition of eating together each night with the younger children. We also have a couple of times a week that we all gather around the table and eat together with the older children.

We make it a point to have family time on a regular basis. Sometimes we grab subs for a picnic in the park. We like to eat at the lake while sitting on a blanket, watching the boats. After we eat dinner, we go for a walk as a family. Family time can be simple or extravagant. We couldn't afford to go on vacation for many years, but when our finances allowed us to, it was another way we used to have family time. Vacation is a great way to get away and focus on your family. Still, if you can't afford to go on vacation, you can make little, inexpensive day trips as we did. We loved to take off and have picnics and spend time together. Having family time builds family closeness and creates those fond memories that our kids can hold onto for the rest of their lives.

Nurturing

A child needs healthy physical touch, kisses, and hugs to feel loved. Babies and toddlers need to be touched and held constantly but as your child gets older, they still need nurturing touch. A teenager may act like they don't want a hug or kiss but I can assure you they need it too.

Nurturing is also comforting your child when they are hurting or needing emotional or physical support. It's important to let your child know you're there to support them when they are hurting. Comforting a younger child is much different than comforting an older one. A young child may need to be held after falling down, but a teenager may need you to sit and talk with them without giving them instructions.

One component of nurturing is helping your child work through areas of fear. Fear comes from things they don't understand. You can recognize symptoms of fear as nervous behaviors, shyness, withdrawal, change in normal behavior patterns, and ongoing feelings of anxiety.

How to nurture:
- Bonding in infancy by comforting, holding, and cuddling
- Hugs and kisses
- Touch on their arm, back, or head
- Rubbing or tickling their back
- Nurturing squeeze on the arm or knee
- Hold them when they are hurt (if they scrape their knee, cut their finger, etc) (opposite of "Rub dirt in it and take a lap" attitude).
- Kiss their booboos
- Sit and listen when they are hurting emotionally.
- Empathize with them and feel their pain.
- Cry with them.
- Let them know it is ok to cry.
- Comfort them by addressing fears with empathy and nurturing vs critical behavior.

Why is Nurturing So Important?
As parents, we need to ensure we give plenty of nurturing love to our children. If they don't get love from us, they will search for it in all the wrong places.

If the mother doesn't show her son love and affection, he will fill that gap with intimate relationships with girls. Visa versa, if a daughter doesn't receive healthy love and attention from her father, she will seek attention from boys and increase the probability of having premarital relations. Lack of parental love creates a void that is so deep that it leaves our kids searching and settling for anyone that makes them feel loved.

In addition to that, the lack of affection in the home most times is translated by kids as parental rejection. This interpretation of rejection can lead our kids outside of the home to find that sense of belonging. Young people will go to extreme measures of joining groups of people that negatively influence them in order to feel a sense of belonging. Also, if a child does not feel loved, instead of coming to us for advice, they will confide in their friends and get advice on the street. We want to be the ones our kids come to for love, attention, and guidance so that we can have a positive impact on their lives.

If you were someone that did not have affection as a child, it might be very difficult for you to show affection to your child, even after a degree of healing. This scenario was the case with me. I knew that I had to push past the awkwardness that I felt and show affection to my children anyway. I needed to practice giving hugs and kisses even if it didn't feel natural. Growing up in a home without affection, you could have embraced the lie that you are just not "that type of person/family." This is not true. God placed the need for affection in all of us; to receive it and give it. It is one of the most essential components of showing His love to one another.

What Would Jesus Do

One of the first lessons God taught me in parenting is to ask the question, "What would Jesus do?" So often, we can decide on a good solution to our parenting situations by asking this question. After all, Jesus is the example that we should all be striving to live by.

I first learned the value of this strategy when we were trying to decide whether we should answer our newborn's cries. We were told with our firstborn to let her cry if her physical needs were met. This response didn't seem to sit right with us. So we started to question this form of parenting.

After my second and third babies were born, we grew into a mindset that we wanted to comfort and nurture our babies instead of letting them cry it out. This presented a battle in my mind and heart because the doctor pointed me in one direction, and my instincts steered me on an opposite course. It was at this point I asked God for wisdom in the situation. He asked me, "What would Jesus do?"

It occurred to me that when we are babies in our faith, Jesus is there to comfort us and help us. He doesn't leave us to work it out. So, I concluded that it was perfectly normal and even good to comfort our babies. Babies need to be snuggled, even if their physical needs are met. Holding them will not "spoil them." As we had more babies, this simple question helped us know the right thing to do. When we comfort our children, bonding occurs.

As a child, I didn't have comfort modeled in my home, so comforting my children did not come naturally. We didn't know what we were doing with our first baby. So we decided to listen to the doctor's instructions. When our babies cried, we now know they needed to be comforted and loved. Now, we understand that they had more needs than just physical. A baby needs to experience the comfort of our words and touch. Also, they need to know we are there to help them feel better when they aren't feeling good emotionally and physically. As our child grew older, we noticed that the "cry it out" method created a deficit in the need for comfort. As a result of this deficit, she grew self-reliant. She became more and more distant and guarded, closing her heart to our attempts to love and help her. She believed that she didn't need anyone to help her as she was used to comforting herself. On a subconscious level, it made her feel like she was all alone and nobody was there to take care of her. Nurturing sets the foundation for the rest of their lives with a feeling of love and security.

When my children were hurt or cried, I didn't know how to comfort them. It felt very awkward. I knew instinctively and by watching other parents that I should do something. Still, it felt foreign. Simple things like touching my children's arms, running my fingers through their hair, caressing their face, rubbing their back, or speaking in a soft nurturing tone were all things that I had to learn how to do. After gaining some healing, I was able to express love for my children more naturally.

Our firstborn is still very independent and tends to feel uncomfortable when we try to love her. She says it's "weird." It breaks my heart as I look at everything we didn't know to do with her. I wish I could turn back the hands of time, hold her, and nurture her from infancy and beyond.

Some other behaviors that you could see if your child has not experienced comfort are eating disorders, addictions, lack of emotions, Obsessive-Compulsive Disorder, control issues, numbness to others' pain, rough and tough exterior, and bullying kids in school.

CHAPTER 8

FINDING THE TREASURES

According to the Bible, God has given us our children to raise and "train them up in the ways (behavior and mentality) they should go." Each of our children has gifts and strengths to be used in this world for God's glory.

This chapter will discuss what we need to do to pull out the gifts that God put inside of our children. We can help or hinder their ability to succeed depending on what we say or do. Therefore, it is crucial to learn how to encourage and support our children to fulfill their God-given purpose and know their identity.

Validation

Regularly verbalizing our approval, affirmation, and appreciation to our children is crucial to their development. When we appreciate our children, we recognize and enjoy their good qualities and accomplishments. We need never assume they know we are proud of them. When we choose to use our words to communicate our appreciation and approval, we affirm who God created them to be. God appointed the father to have the loudest voice in the family structure to activate the child's identity. However, the mother has a part to play in this as well. Our tone of voice and words must be filtered through affirmation and approval. Guidance can be misinterpreted as rejection if correction is not done with an affirming undertone.

If a child has not been validated and affirmed, they will be insecure about who they are. This insecurity can cause them to follow the crowd instead of sticking to their values. Insecurity can also cause a lack of confidence in so many areas of life. For example, as a child grows into a teenager and then an adult lacking affirmation, they will work to gain approval from various sources (some may not be healthy). Also, a college student who has never been validated or affirmed may jump from one career path to another, trying to figure out what they are good at.

Examples of ways you can validate your child:
- Look for ways to praise them.
- Look for ways to compliment them.
- Always let them know they did a good job.
- Pray for God to show you their natural abilities.
- Pray God shows you their strengths and gifts.
- Pray God shows you their purpose so that you can identify their skill sets.
- As God reveals their skill sets and strengths, verbalize them to your child.
- Identify and verbalize their God-given gifts and strengths.
- Verbally acknowledge when they do the right thing and use good character.
- Frequently tell them you are proud of them.
- Look for times to verbally acknowledge their integrity.
- Point out specific examples in a job well done.
- Look for situations to say, "Good job," and, "Thank you," even in the little things.
- Acknowledge improvement in behaviors.
- Acknowledge improvement in school grades.

Your Words

While the tone we use with our children is important, the words that we speak over our children are crucial. Words can either bless them or curse them, bring life or death in their life and heart.

Proverbs 18:21 NKJV tells us, *"Death and life are in the power of the tongue."*

Matthew 12:33-37 NLT Jesus is talking, saying, *"A tree is identified by its fruit. If a tree is good, its fruit will be good. If a tree is bad, its fruit will be bad. You brood of snakes! How could evil men like you speak what is good and right? For whatever is in your heart determines what you say. A good person produces good things from the treasury of a good heart, and an evil person produces evil things from the treasury of an evil heart. And I tell you this, you must give an account on judgment day for every idle word you speak. The words you say will either acquit you or condemn you."*

In this part of scripture, Jesus is talking about knowing a tree by its fruit (what people say or do). As we deal with the wounds and pain in our hearts, we will produce good fruit. On the other hand, if we stay in our wounded state, responding out of triggers and bad fruit, we can cause serious damage to ourselves and others. Our words and actions expose the condition of the heart: *"Out of the abundance of the heart, the mouth speaks,"* Luke 6:45.

Good words and actions come from a good heart. This scripture is powerful to understand regarding parenting because we will all give an account of everything we say, good or bad, on Judgement day. How much more important is it that we will give an account of what we say to our children? These are the ones that God has entrusted us to love, nurture, and train up. Our words and our actions (our fruit) directly impact the fruit of our children.

When we speak negative words to and over our children, the enemy can take these words and cause them to be true. Proverbs 15:4 ESV states, *"A gentle tongue is a tree of life, but perverseness in it breaks the spirit."*

Our children believe what we tell them. If we say things like, "What is wrong with you, can't you do anything right?," they are going to believe that something is wrong with them. If we tell our children, "You will never amount to anything," they are going to believe that. These words are examples of speaking death (physical, emotional, and spiritual) over our children.

On the other hand, if we call out the positive things we see in our children, even though their behavior is less than perfect, it will do the opposite and bring life. When we affirm in them how God sees them, it causes them to become that.

Proud Father

My husband took our boys on a church camping trip. On the first day, it was stormy. The tent had a hole in the top of it, directly over my middle son's sleeping bag. By the time they went to bed, his sleeping bag was drenched. Our middle son was so upset that he started crying. Then, unexpectedly, our oldest son piped up and said, "Josiah, why don't you take my sleeping bag, and I will sleep in yours?" This behavior was so out of character for my oldest son that it surprised everyone. Eli's helpfulness so touched my husband that the next morning he praised him in front of everybody. When they got home, my husband started bragging about it at the dinner table before the whole family. My son's face lit up! He was so happy and proud of himself. My husband's affirmation and public declarations spoke volumes to my son's heart and his sense of self-worth. Leading up to this, we intentionally built him up with affirming words and praise. We were trying to shift his negative behaviors of self-centeredness. So along with teaching him about being selfless, we also looked for ways to affirm the positive things he did.

When we encourage and praise our kids, it lifts their confidence and brings them to a higher level in themselves and God. Now I'm not saying that we aren't supposed to correct and tell them what they are doing wrong, but the words we choose and the way we speak make the difference in whether we are speaking life or death over them. Our kids will live up to whatever we expect of them and what we are telling them.

Let Them Know

It is essential to verbalize to our kids that they are important. Josiah, my sixth born, had saved up his money to buy a nice bike. As he got it home and put it together, he realized it was defective. He was devastated as he had worked so hard and long to get this bike. Josiah wanted us to take him to the store to exchange it sooner than later. We were trying hard to accommodate this half-hour trip to the store plus the time it would take to load it into our van. We explained to him that we needed to take him on the weekend in order to have plenty of time before the store closed for the day. Somewhere lost in communication, my son thought he wasn't important enough for us to take the time to drive the distance to return his bike. Do you see how the enemy will use the littlest things to twist the truth into a lie and warp our kids' thinking? The weekend finally came. My husband and I were talking out loud, making our plans for the day. We listed all the errands that we had to run. My son heard us making plans. He thought we had forgotten to add his bike return to our list of things to do and said, "Since we might be close to that side of town for your errands, do you think we can take my bike back to the store?" My husband and I both heard it at the same time. We could hear the tone of his voice and his choice of words that he didn't think we felt his needs were important enough to prioritize his bike return, just for him. My husband quickly corrected him and said:

"Buddy, we already planned to take you to the store today." Then my husband added, "We don't need a separate reason to go out of our way, to take you to the store because you are worth it and are important to us."

This small moment made a significant impact on my son's heart. The look on his face revealed that he was almost ready to cry in response to what was just said. That day, the lie of "I'm not valued" was uprooted. Instead, the truth of worth and value was deeply planted in his heart. As we allow the Holy Spirit to show us areas to better fill our kids' emotional cups, He will do just that. If we acknowledge Him, He will direct our path, even in parenting.

Perfectionism

It is important that our kids know they are appreciated for a job well done. One of the mistakes I made as a parent was functioning out of perfectionism. Up until I gained healing, I embraced perfectionism as a good thing. I wrapped up perfectionism in the package of "being excellent" or an "overachiever." I gained the reputation of someone who was reliable, efficient, and a performer. This mentality spilled over into my children. I expected "excellence" (perfection) from myself, and I also expected it from my children. Everything I did was never good enough for my standards, and I continually worked on making things better. I had to try harder and harder, perfecting the way I did everything. As I taught my children to do something, I instructed them out of an expectancy of "excellence," but what I called "excellence" was an unobtainable level of accomplishment. The problem was that they got the message that they couldn't ever do things well enough to please me and meet my expectations. As I expected such a high level of performance, the bar was always moved higher and higher, meaning my kids could never hit the mark of "good enough." This left them feeling unappreciated and believing that they were never going to be good enough.

Encouragement is Necessary

Encouragement is necessary to set your child on the path to success as an adult. With parental encouragement, a child has hope, inspiration, and confidence to attain their goals.

Parenting isn't only about instructing; it's about encouraging as well. Ask God to help you see areas where your child needs encouragement. Even when instructing our kids, we can encourage them.

As you encourage, it's important to support your child in his or her endeavors and his or her weaknesses. Support is most needed in the pre-teen and teen years. This means to come alongside and give emotional and physical support as your child learns to navigate different things in life. As you support your teen, they will feel like they can trust you, share their struggles with you, and allow you to speak into their life.

Without encouragement and support, your child may lack self-confidence to accomplish their goals and may fall into the trap of giving up easily on projects they start. A perpetuation of not accomplishing things can cause feelings of failure and frustration. This cycle can cause them to develop a lack of motivation and initiative that will follow into adulthood.

Definition: Encouragement — 1) The action of giving someone support, confidence, or hope. 2) Persuasion to do or to continue something. 3) The act of trying to stimulate the development of an activity, state, or belief. (Oxford Advanced Learner's Dictionary)

Ways to encourage your child:

- Encourage them with ideas to practice their natural God-given gifts.
- Focus on the desired behavior to encourage them to be the best version of themselves.
- Believe in their abilities and verbalize them.
- Be their biggest "cheerleader."
- Help them know God desires for them to succeed.
- Encourage them when they get frustrated to keep going.
- Teach them that mistakes and failures are all part of the learning process to succeed.
- Tell them they can do it.
- Teach them a task, oversee it, and then praise them when it is accomplished.
- Help them learn time management.
- Help them set goals.
- Gently give guidance without control.
- Speak words that share your confidence in their ability to get through tough times.
- Teach them that failing is part of succeeding.
- Encourage them to keep trying when they don't succeed.
- Listen intently to their concerns.
- Walk alongside them as they learn new things.

- Reassure them that you are there for them.
- Let them know you are on their side and you have their backs.
- Communicate that you are for them and not against them.
- Demonstrate how to do a task, do it with them, and then encourage them as they do it on their own.
- Stand by your older children as they deal with the challenges of becoming adults.
- Be their advocate, making sure their teachers and caregivers are encouraging and supportive as well.

Encouraging Younger Children

One typical day in our house, my boys were treating each other poorly and acting like enemies. All the bickering and fighting wore me down, and my patience was running thin. I called my older son over to me as I noticed he was the common denominator of the fighting. I braced myself and reset my attitude from being annoyed to knowing that I needed to speak into my son's heart. I knew if I could speak to his heart, we could get to the root of the problem. So many times, we want the behavior to go away without finding the root cause. Unfortunately, this only gives a temporary fix to the wrong behaviors. We talked about what was bothering him, got to the cause of his frustration, and dealt with it. I then used the situation to encourage his heart. I declared and told him that I knew he was a sweet, kind boy and wasn't acting like himself today. Instead of pointing to the negative, I encouraged and called him to behave how we would expect him to. Notice, I didn't tell him how bad he was acting. I focused on how I knew he could behave in that situation. If we establish that expectation for our kids and how they are supposed to behave, they will live up to it. Setting positive expectations while giving warm encouragement has a powerful effect on our child's behavior.

We need to look for ways to encourage our kids in the little things and the big things. If they know we are on their side and cheering them on, we will win their hearts. As we encourage our kids they feel like we are on their side, and it creates a closeness between our kids and us.

Natural Abilities

My oldest son has a natural ability to make useful items out of scraps. My husband and I have been amazed at some of the things he has created that actually work and can be used. He loves to spend days at a time thinking and planning how to build something. Then, he finds his materials and spends hours making them. Nobody taught him how to do this. He just started analyzing how things were made. One day he said, "I can make that." And so, he did.

As we see this natural ability in him, we tell him what a good job he does and look for ways to teach him how to hone his skills. He wants to get better at what he does so he can sell his projects, so we are careful to encourage him in his ambitious plans.

He makes a big mess and gets into my husband's tools all the time. This can be frustrating, but we know that we can't squelch this passion and gift in him. There is a fine line to walk when we encourage and cultivate these gifts in our children while gently teaching them life lessons.

As he shifted from making items to trying to sell them, we had a whole new level of training that needed to occur. Sometimes, we must reign him in and teach him what would and wouldn't be appropriate and redirected his thinking a little bit. Sometimes he wants to jump ahead of himself, and we have to redirect him.

Recognizing natural gifts in our children and encouraging them in those abilities is like putting lighter fluid on their fire. Your opinion of them matters more than any other person in their life. When you encourage them and see their abilities, it gives them the confidence to go after their dreams and goals. This, coupled with biblical guidance causes them to be unstoppable in their God-given purpose in life.

Evidence of Support

One day, my daughter Arriah and I went on a leisurely walk, spending some much-needed time together. Our walk turned into a heartfelt conversation as she brought up some challenging times she had recently gone through. She explained the effects of my supportive words during that low point in her spiritual journey. Arriah had felt defeated and like she couldn't measure up to God's expectations in this situation. She felt so discouraged that she almost gave up on her faith. She shared that if my response had been a tone of what she was doing wrong rather than of support, she wouldn't have felt the strength to prevail over it. As she shared her heart, I realized how crucial it was that I did not speak out of what my natural eyes saw, instead keeping my eyes on how God saw her. Back when she was struggling, I reminded her of God's purposes for her life and all the great things I knew she would accomplish if she kept her eyes fixed on Him. Further, I explained that I believed in her ability to rise above this and reminded her of the things she needed to overcome. In this, I gained a deeper understanding of how vital it is to help our children see themselves and their situation as God sees it, especially amid life's challenges.

Don't be Pushy

As our kids learn new skills, we need to support them without pushing our agenda on them. We've all seen the parents that live vicariously through their children and push them to do things out of their own shortcomings. Parents can have an overwhelming desire for their kids to start where they left off. Let's say, for instance, the father has his own business as a contractor, and he wants his son to take over his business someday. The father pushes his son to learn his trade and do his work, but the son has no talent or interest in this field. As the father does this, it causes the child to be frustrated and communicates a false identity. As the son struggles with mistaken identity, he will struggle with feelings of confusion and failure that will hinder him from knowing who God created him to be. We need to recognize that God made each of our children unique with a specific purpose in mind. Our job is to watch and listen as God reveals those things and help our children walk in their own divine callings. As parents, we need to gently guide and encourage our children in their strengths and interests while giving them the direction, confidence, encouragement, and ability to make decisions.

Digging Up the Treasure

We can do things to help our children discover their purposes, gifts and talents, which will help them establish their own identities. When our kids are young, we can expose them to stimulating, interesting, and engaging experiences. The experiences can include reading, arts and crafts, projects, musical instruments, and sports. As we expose our children to these things, we can observe what interests them most and assess their natural skills and abilities. As we see our child's God-given abilities and passions, we need to encourage our children verbally and physically in those areas. As our children grow, we also need to continue to pray that God shows us any hidden gifts that we need to cultivate. God put these gifts in our children, and He is so faithful to guide us as we ask for wisdom. Finding the treasures in our children may take some digging, but we must find them. We must keep our eyes open to see that "diamond in the rough." As we uncover and speak to the treasure that God placed inside them, they will enter into adulthood with confidence, knowing their identity and their purpose.

CHAPTER 9

TRAINING UP OUR CHILDREN

Sometimes parenting is enjoyable and rewarding, but other times it is daunting. I admit that I'm not a perfect parent, and no matter how hard I try, I never will be. However, we need to have our foundation of parenting rooted in our Heavenly Father. God is the best example we could ever have, especially for those who have not had the best parental examples growing up. With God as our leader and consistency in our approach, we can tackle all that lies ahead.

Our goal in training our children is to help them grow into responsible, dependable, trustworthy adults who have good morals, values, and integrity. We want our children to be adults that we can be proud of. The goal is to help them establish self-control without controlling them. We want them to be good husbands, wives, employees/employers to glorify God in everything they do and to be productive and responsible citizens in God's kingdom. We also want to enjoy our children while they are growing up. Therefore, we do our best to create a peaceful, loving environment in our homes. Training our children is a process, and we'll never arrive at a destination of perfect children. However, suppose we are diligent and faithful in teaching them God's love. In that case, our children will grow and be great assets to our family, society, and God's kingdom.

Our number one priority is to teach and model to our children God's word and His unconditional love. They need to know what the Bible says and be able to apply it to their lives. If children believe they are only accountable to Mom and Dad, they might not hold on to their good behavioral patterns when they are out of our sight. On the other hand, when they realize God loves them and has expectations for them, it helps enforce our rules and boundaries. Also, if our children understand that God is watching over them even when we can't see them, it keeps them more accountable. It is essential that we build a good foundation of our faith and our beliefs into our children. To establish this, our family does a daily devotion with our children. We teach them the word of God in practical everyday things, and we live out the example for them to see in us.

Foundation Built on the Word

Asking the question, "What would Jesus do?" sets the precedence of referring to Jesus and God's word for all of our parenting needs. In training up our children, we have the perfect manual—God's word—for teaching them. The Bible is the perfect foundation for teaching our children everything they need to know to survive and thrive in this world.

We won't always be there for them later on in life. However, if we establish God's word in them at a young age, they will be able to use the biblical guidance on their own. The Bible also creates a common foundation of principles for everyone in the family to build on. Everyone knows the boundaries and standards that are required of them.

As we go through the day and things come up, we can always point our children to scripture for direction. For example, one of our boys, in particular, has a problem with complaining. So we explain to him that God says in the Bible that we aren't supposed to complain.

Philippians 2:14 NLT says, *"Do everything without complaining and arguing."*

Sometimes we read the scriptures from the Bible. Other times, we quote it and explain them to our children. We even have our children sit and write the scripture out to imprint the words in their hearts. I put scriptures on notecards and post them on the refrigerator so that everyone can see them. This helps everyone remember what God says about a particular issue. If we, as parents, have the scripture memorized and can speak the scripture to our child, it is very powerful.

Hebrews 4:12 NLT says, *"For the word of God is alive and powerful. It is sharper than any two-edged sword, cutting between soul and spirit, between joint and marrow. It exposes our innermost thoughts and desires."*

When we speak the Word of God to our children while they act on their sinful nature, it cuts straight to the core of the issues and helps them get their thoughts and attitudes straightened out. I remember the first time I actually tried this. One of my children was misbehaving, and I spoke a scripture of correction to them. Their behavior changed instantly!

I never thought just speaking the word of God would make that much of a difference, but let me tell you, it made a huge difference. I continue to speak scripture whenever my children's behavior is inappropriate. The Bible gives our children "the why" of how we need to behave. If we do not establish the proper authority for our morals and values, who is to say what's right and wrong? When we point our children to the word of God, it's not just what Mom and Dad says that goes. It's a much higher authority than that—it's all about what God says.

Also, when Mom and Dad set the example and live according to the Bible, children follow the example. All kids want boundaries and standards established so that they can gain confidence when they meet them. In addition, it gives them a sense of security and accomplishment.

Teach by Doing

We can use everyday life experiences to teach and train our children. I have found that the life lessons learned by experience stick best in their minds. For instance, when we went to the mall as a family, we often saw a homeless man. We gave some money to one of our younger children and instructed him to give it to the homeless man. We explained to our kids that this man didn't have a home and probably didn't have people to love him. We made a decision, as a family, to get to know this man and show God's love to him. The next time we saw him at the mall, we found out his name. He was shocked that someone wanted to know his name and talk with him. Time after time, we visited Dale at the mall, bringing him a few dollars for food. My kids learned to be generous and live the part in the Bible that talked about Christians being God's hands and feet to the poor.

In Matthew 25:35 NLT Jesus says, *"For I was hungry, and you fed me. I was thirsty, and you gave me a drink. I was a stranger, and you invited me into your home."* In this passage, the disciples were asking Jesus when they did these things for him. In verse 40, Jesus says, *"And the King will say, I tell you the truth, when you did it to one of the least of these my brothers and sisters, you were doing it to me!"*

We were teaching our children to value this homeless man even though he appeared to be one of the "least of these." Then, one frigid winter night in upstate New York, we saw Dale walking along, shivering and trying to keep warm. We stopped our car and invited him to stay with us for the night. Dale was elated to come home with us. As a family, we gave him some hot home-cooked food and visited with him.

Dale didn't smell or look nice, but we taught our children to look past that and love him anyway. Dale needed to see God's unconditional love through each of us. We rescued Dale from the bitter weather many times over, including on Thanksgiving and during some of our family Christmas cookie-making nights.

I think that this was one of the most valuable lessons we could have taught our children. Through the experiences with Dale, they truly learned to be witnesses of Christ's unconditional love, have compassion for the less fortunate, and they learned how to make a difference in this world. We have since moved out of the area, and we pray for Dale often. We got attached to him, and he to us. I don't know for sure, but I often wonder if we were the only family experience he ever had.

Ask for Wisdom

Asking God for wisdom in challenging situations is an excellent habit to get into.

James 1:5 NKJV says, *"If any of you lacks wisdom, let him ask of God, who gives to all liberally and without reproach, and it will be given to him."*

So many times I've faced situations with one of my kids that I didn't know how to deal with. In a quick moment, I'd think of all the books I've read, the parenting classes I attended, all the past experiences I've had, and still, I was clueless about what to do.

It is in these moments I stop and ask, "Lord, give me wisdom in this situation." Father God knows our children better than we know them. He knows all the hidden things in their heart and their struggles. He also knows the solutions to the problems they face. When we ask for His wisdom, it opens the opportunity for God to unlock those secrets about our children so we can help them. Parenting is not easy, and sometimes our parenting manuals won't have the answers we need. But God always has the answers. Simply ask for wisdom, and He will freely give it.

Adjust Their Attitude

Teaching our children to have a good attitude and good character is important. A bad attitude is one of the biggest things that get us in trouble in life. Teaching our children the scriptures in the Bible about attitude is a good place to start in helping them maintain a positive attitude.

Definition: Attitude— 1) A settled way of thinking or feeling about someone or something, typically one that is reflected in a person's behavior. 2) A position of the body proper to or implying an action or mental state. 3) Uncooperative behavior; a resentful or antagonistic manner. (Oxford Advanced Learner's Dictionary)

Definition: Character—1) The mental and moral qualities distinctive to an individual. 2) The quality of being individual, typically in an interesting or unusual way 3) Strength and originality in a person's nature 4) A person's good reputation (Oxford Advanced Learner's Dictionary)

Scriptures about attitude:
Philippians 2:14-15 NKJV *"Do all things without grumbling and complaining, that you may become blameless and harmless, children of*

God without fault in the midst of a crooked and perverse generation, among whom you shine as lights in the world."

Colossians 3:23 NLT *"Work willingly at whatever you do, as though you were working for the Lord rather than for people."*

James 4:10 NLT *"Humble yourselves in the sight of the Lord, and He will lift you up."*

Having a good attitude in life makes life go well, and everyone around us responds to us more positively. One important lesson we've tried so hard to instill in our children is to focus on the positive things of each situation. Focusing on the positives and the rewards of the outcome helps us adjust our attitude. For example, when my child does an excellent job with a good attitude, that child is rewarded. The same applies to adults. When we do things with a good (willing) attitude (as unto the Lord), we get rewarded through God's blessings. Remember, our goal is to train our children to become adults who glorify God in all they do. God says that if we live without grumbling and complaining, we will be harmless, blameless, without fault, and be a light in this perverse world. We want our children to shine in all they do, so we need to teach them to have good attitudes.

The Value of Humility

Being humble is a part of having a good attitude. Nobody likes to hear someone bragging about themselves or putting themselves above others. Being humble is the opposite of esteeming yourself higher than others.

Definition: Humility— A modest or low view of one's own importance; humbleness (Oxford Advanced Learner's Dictionary)

Philippians 2:3 ESV says, *"Do nothing from rivalry or conceit, but in humility count others more significant than yourselves."*

I want my children to treat their siblings with the attitude that their siblings are more important than they are. Suppose everyone treats others as more important than themselves. In that case, we reduce conflict and increase peace because pride is what causes arguments.

Jesus was talking to his disciples and explained to them in Mark 9:35 NKJV, *"And He sat down, called the twelve, and said to them, "If anyone desires to be first, he shall be last of all and servant of all."*

Jesus was saying that if you put yourself first, you will be last. But if you humble yourself and become a servant, you will be first in the kingdom of Heaven. So as we teach our children to be humble, we teach them to be good servants.

By teaching them to be good servants, we are preparing them to be good leaders. The Bible explains that if you learn how to be a good servant, God can appoint you as a leader. Therefore, I look for opportunities to help my children learn to be good servants and practice humility.

I always tell them to think of others before they think of themselves. When I notice one of my children is trying to get ahead of their siblings, I make that child go last. I try to live out what the scriptures say by example and help my children do the same in everything. The values that we are trying to instill in our children take time. Even when we think they've gotten it, they'll remind us that it is a process. We need to teach it through childhood. They constantly need to be reminded of the morals and values we want them to live by.

Humility helps us show respect and honor. These are essential character traits to teach our children.

Exodus 20:12 NLT says, *"Honor your father and mother. Then you will live a long, full life in the land the Lord your God is giving you."*

First and foremost, we need to teach our children to honor us as parents. Their relationship with us is foundational for how they will treat others outside the home. We teach our children how to respect and honor by showing respect and honor. We teach the appropriate way to talk and respond to other adults and even their peers.

Romans 12:10 ESV says, *"Love one another with brotherly affection. Outdo one another in showing honor."*

The honor and respect that our children learn will help them go further in life. Their solid character will help them glorify God and shine above most of their peers in adulthood.

Tune Your Tone

The tone of voice is a huge factor in our house. If the tone of voice is "off," it's a clear indication the attitude is "off" as well. When our children speak to us or one another, and there is an abrasiveness, loudness, or rudeness in their voice, we know there's something wrong. Using a kind tone in our voice can show honor and respect to others. On the contrary, using a harsh tone can show disrespect.

The tone of our voice sets the tone for the conversation. Have you ever been texting or emailing someone and misunderstood someone's heart because you weren't able to hear the tone of their voice? I believe our tone adds meaning to our words. You can say the exact words but create a totally different meaning just by changing your tone. If our children have an inappropriate tone in their voice, we will simply tell them to listen to their voice and change their tone. If it continues, it alerts us that there is a deeper reason for the tone, then we will sit down to talk to the child. We figure out the root cause and get to the heart of the problem.

In order to respond to your child with God's type of love, you need to allow God to heal and change your heart. I pray that God uses this book as the roadmap along your journey to healing and better parenting.

The Value of Responsibilities

Building responsibility and a solid work ethic in our children is crucial. We assign chores to each child who lives in our house when they are old enough to help. Giving our children chores and responsibilities helps them grow into responsible adults. Nobody wants to marry a young man or woman who doesn't know how to be responsible and productive in life. If we don't teach our children to work hard and be responsible when they are young, they won't just wake up one day and say, "Oh, I think I'll start working hard and be responsible." Working hard is a learned behavior, and it's learned over some time.

One of my boys has a more challenging time than the others practicing a good work ethic. He complains, cuts corners, and gives us a hard time working around the house. Up until a point, we expected him to take out the trash daily and load the dishwasher occasionally. One day, I asked God for wisdom because his lack of ambition concerned me. God's response to me was to give him more responsibility and make him work more. He needed to get more practice and get used to working. I obeyed, and it has worked like a charm. We started asking him to do jobs like cleaning areas in the house, mowing the lawn, cleaning the yard, stacking wood, etc. This child is becoming a great worker. I also remind this child about what the Bible says about laziness. There are several scriptures on laziness, here are a few: Proverbs 13:4 NLT says, *"Lazy people want much but get little, but those who work hard will prosper."*

Colossians 3:23 ESV says, *"Whatever you do, work heartily, as for the Lord and not for men."*

Proverbs 18:9 NLT says, *"A lazy person is as bad as someone who destroys things."*

Set Family Rules

Each of us needs to decide which rules to establish in our households. Look at the Biblical guidelines for Christian behavior and go from there. There are things that I may not allow in my family, but you may think they are perfectly fine. If we yield to God's word and His voice and ask Him for wisdom, we can establish a good foundation for our household rules and guidelines.

As you establish the rules for your family, talk about them, make sure everyone understands them, and have consequences for breaking the rules. There are times when we need to put our foot down, and there are times when we need to extend grace. This is all a matter of godly wisdom and discernment.

Know Your Children's Friends

We also are cautious with whom our kids hang out with. I've noticed that when our children are acting up more than usual, I suspect their friends are influencing their behavior. We are the company that we keep and we become who we hang around.

Even as an adult, if I am hanging out with a negative, gossipy person, I notice those same behaviors show up in my life. Children are even more vulnerable and impressionable than adults. We can't expect that our kids are going to hang out with a rebellious friend without consequences. If you detect something that is "off" in your child's behavior, start investigating who they are hanging out with.

My daughter had a close friend who was influencing her attitudes, perceptions, and behavior. My daughter, age 14, had this best friend for a couple of years. So, I was slow to catch on to the problem. I prayed for this daughter and talked with her for a while, and I still saw no improvement.

Then, I began to pray for wisdom in the situation. My daughter was depressed and irritable. She started talking about not wanting to live. This wasn't like her. Things were stable in our household, and all the other kids were very happy and enjoying life. I couldn't understand why my daughter was so depressed. After praying for wisdom, God answered me very quickly. Looking back, I don't know why it took me so long to ask Him! God revealed to me that this particular friend was influencing my daughter negatively.

This friend of hers was a strong Christian, so I didn't suspect that she would negatively influence my daughter. However, after talking to my daughter, I realized this friend had severe issues with depression. The friend's outlook on life was significantly distorted by the turmoil going on in her home. This depressive state and perception of life rubbed off onto my daughter, even though she wasn't struggling with the same things. It was almost like the depressed attitude was contagious.

I told my daughter that she had to stop spending time with her friend for awhile until we could figure things out. We prayed with her and broke any influence of spiritual issues she had from this friendship. Within a couple of days, my daughter made a dramatic change for the better. She was like a new person. Her depression lifted, and she had a completely different outlook on life. Her attitude towards family was better, and she was thriving. I can tell you several other stories, but the moral of the story is that as parents, we need to be in tune with our kids to help them navigate through life's challenges. Those challenges include helping them guard their hearts with their friendships.

Romantic Relationships

Teaching our children about friendships includes boy/girl friendships and relationships. When our children are young, we teach them that the "boyfriend, girlfriend" relationships are reserved for when people are old enough to start thinking about marriage. When our children are young, we monitor their entertainment. We discourage our kids from watching television programs that promote preteens and teens kissing and inappropriate affection outside a serious relationship leading to marriage. We call our way of thinking "dating with a purpose" or courting.

Our thoughts are based on the principle that our children should not be thinking about a boyfriend/girlfriend relationship until they are mature enough to handle it. That means that emotionally, mentally, and spiritually, they need to understand and deal with this level of relationship responsibility. When our kids have a boy/girl relationship before they are ready, they give pieces of their hearts away to someone they might not marry. In giving pieces of their heart away, our children get wounded by the relationships. Then, when they are ready to get married, they have a broken, wounded, or partial heart to give to their husband/wife.

We must teach our children to wait for that relationship until they are emotionally ready to become husbands or wives to preserve their hearts and innocence. Boy/girl relationships put our children in a vulnerable position to fall into sexual temptations that would not be pleasing to God. Giving in to temptation wounds them further. It is easy for them to fall into temptation with raging hormones, thus negatively affecting their lives.

Timing Matters

Knowing the right timing for boyfriend/girlfriend relationships is essential. We talk to our kids often about how to gauge the timing of entering into a possible relationship. They need to ask God and themselves: Is this possibly the one God wants me to be with for a lifetime?

Timing is one of the main factors that determine whether or not the marriage will last. If we get involved in a relationship too early, even when we are mature enough, it can still cause problems. For example, I rushed the process of marriage quicker than I know God wanted me to. In my first year of college, I became impatient. I just wanted to get married, which led me to make decisions before God's appointed timing. This caused my husband and me to go through challenges that we wouldn't have had to go through if we had waited for God's timing.

Now that I'm a mother, I realize I wasn't ready for marriage, and I should've taken things a lot slower. But, it was that longing for love that caused me to get ahead of schedule. I thank God that He worked it all out for good because even though I was in a hurry to get married, I ended up getting married to a really good guy. It could've ended up differently, however, because I didn't know my husband very well before marrying him. He could've turned out to be someone that wasn't so good for me.

CHAPTER 10

BUILDING BLOCKS FOR A STRONG FOUNDATION

L ike building a house, there are layers and stages of building an emotional foundation in childhood. If each stage is built strong, the child will grow into a confident, secure adult who knows their purpose and identity. Just like the foundation of a house, if the previous layer or stage hasn't been appropriately laid, the next level will be faulty. Each one of these stages builds on the one prior. As the first stage is built solid and stable, then you can build the second stage, and so on. Each stage hinges on the previous, preparing the child to withstand the challenging winds and stresses of life as they grow older and into adulthood. Each layer of the foundation is naturally laid as consistent love and nurturing are given from the parents.

The first stage of the foundation is basic trust. This level is built as the child is born and should be established from birth to two years old. Trust begins as bonding occurs and continues as parents nurture their baby daily. Nurturing touch is the main ingredient in building this first layer of emotional foundation. Each day, trust is established as you gently touch, hug, kiss, and hold your baby. Warm tones of voice and nurturing responses to the baby's cries and needs also create trust in the child at this stage. Then, as you love your child unconditionally, requiring nothing from them, they simply receive your love.

Earlier I shared that before we knew any better we let our first baby cry it out and self soothe. As we did this, our daughter wasn't able to establish this initial foundation of trust and this also affected her ability to form the subsequent stages properly. It affected her ability to become independent and individuate with confidence as a preschooler and even on up through high school. She struggled with the confidence in making decisions and knowing her identity and purpose as she became an adult.

The second foundational stage is autonomy, which begins between ages 2-4. If a child feels like they are safe and loved, this stage is established. Suppose a child feels the parent's unconditional love and approval. In that case, they will have the confidence to start developing their sense of independence from their parents. The autonomy stage is built when a child begins to learn how to do things for themselves.

It is also at this point the child begins to lean on the sense of security that should have already been established. The stability will help them feel safe while being separated from their parents for some time in different environments like a playgroup, at the playground, preschool, or church nursery. But again, the sense of security is developed from the consistency in routines, boundaries, and nurturing up to this point.

During the autonomy stage, if a child feels approval, they will begin to exercise their uniqueness in the way they feel, think, and act. As a child begins to exercise his or her God-given differences, he or she needs to have the freedom to say, "No, I don't like that," or, "No, I don't want that." As parents, we need to determine whether or not the child is acting out of rebellion or establishing independence. Always disciplining for a "no" response will not allow the child to grow in this stage of development. Also, this is when a child needs to feel safe saying "no" to uncomfortable situations. Being taught and having the permission to say "no" to the affection that doesn't feel right can help that child feel safe and secure in their decisions. The permission to say "no" may also keep them safe in a dangerous or inappropriate situation later in life, if one arises.

For example:

- Uncle Fred demands a hug and kiss from Anna.
- Anna is saying no and is not comfortable hugging and kissing Uncle Fred.
- Anna is made to give a hug or kiss anyway.
- Anna was just taught that it is not okay to set healthy boundaries even when she doesn't feel comfortable giving affection to a person.
- Contrary to this example, if a child can decide only to reciprocate affection that feels appropriate, they will form healthy boundaries and confidence to say "no" to inappropriate affection if it arises.

Some ways to help establish independence:

- Exercise patience, and allow your child to do things for themselves with supervision (make a sandwich, zip their jacket, etc.).
- Allow them to explore in safe areas.
- Allow them to make simple decisions (pick out three outfits and let them choose one for the day).
- Allow opportunities for self-care (brushing teeth, brushing hair, etc.).
- Give them little jobs to do (feed the dog, wipe off table, help set the table).
- Let them speak for themselves (ordering at a restaurant, answering when asked a question).
- Don't get upset when mistakes or messes are made.
- Give them choices.

The third stage is when they learn their individualism, which should take place between 4-6 years old. Individuation is similar to autonomy, but this next stage is when the child starts to step into their uniqueness even more. Becoming an individual is demonstrated in personality, character, and identity. As a child knows they are approved of and accepted, they are confident to embrace the traits that make them unique without fearing rejection.

In the autonomy stage (2-4), a child may want to dress themself. As they enter the individuation stage (4-6), they also will have preferences in regard to colors, styles, and combinations of the outfit they want to wear. For example, a mother only allows Suzy to wear natural colors, but Suzy likes bright and sparkly clothes. One day, Suzy demonstrates (with strong emotions) her preference to wear a pretty bright pink shirt like her friend Anna. To help strengthen individuation in this situation, the mother can take Suzy to the store and help her pick out some clothing that better suits her preference. Suppose Suzy is not allowed to exercise her unique taste in clothing. In that case, she could be hindered from developing a solid self-perception and self-confidence, keeping her from embracing her differences as an individual. Suzy may comply after a battle for the moment. As a young adult with newly found freedom, Suzy may then overcompensate (acting like a six-year-old) by wearing neon colors to a job interview. If Suzy had been allowed to individuate earlier on, she wouldn't feel like she had to prove her uniqueness in a rebellious way later in life.

During this phase of development, a child is starting to learn boundaries. A child expressing his or her uniqueness can be one factor that helps them grasp this valuable life lesson. If a child can say, "No, I don't like that," at this stage, it helps them learn how to set boundaries and be confident in their right to do so. If a child has not felt like their opinion or feelings are valued, they will struggle to set boundaries throughout life. The fourth foundational stage is formed between the ages of 6-12. As a child gains confidence in who they are and in their abilities, they will grow into the initiative stage. Encouragement is needed most in this stage. Encouragement is required in order to help the child feel the confidence and desire to stretch past their comfort zone and try new things.

When children know their parents approve of them, they know they have the unconditional support. They know that they can make mistakes without judgment or rejection, giving them as sense of security without fearing failure. Mistakes can be made and learned from. If a child does not feel approval, they may fail and then not have the courage to get back up and try new things. Suppose the initiative stage of emotional development has not been reached. In that case, your child may be a creative thinker but never take the initiative and develop this creative gifting. Helping your child set and accomplish goals is essential at this time. At this point, a child will grow in their abilities and confidence, achieving more and more significant milestones. As they achieve a level of success and are using the gifts and talents God has given them, they can then reach the next level of growth in pursuing their purpose. If this foundation is laid in these early years, they will have an optimistic outlook and believe they can achieve great things.

The fifth stage of emotional development is the social development stage and should occur between the ages of 12-18. This stage is when preteens and teens begin to cultivate friends and groups of people they enjoy. If the family relationship was healthy, the teen will feel secure in their identity and be drawn to healthy relationships with similar values. They will know what groups they belong to and what groups they don't and make wise choices accordingly. Suppose a child's emotional needs for affection, acceptance, affirmation, and appreciation have been met. In that case, a teenager will be able to choose between healthy and unhealthy relationships without fearing rejection.

As emotional needs have been met at home, a teenager will not fear voicing his or her morals and convictions to peers. They can say no to something harmful and not be fearful of being rejected. If the need for approval has been met, the fear of rejection does not dictate bad decisions. A secure family gives a teenager the strength and confidence to say "no" to peer pressure. Suppose parents have given the emotional support required for each of the previous stages of emotional development. In that case, they can trust their teenager to make healthy relationship decisions.

Teens will venture outside the family to find who they are and where they belong if they haven't felt entirely accepted and affirmed at home. This is when teenagers join friend groups that are unhealthy. A peer group of teenagers that doesn't feel loved and supported at home tends to be unsafe, angry, and rebellious. They also gravitate towards other teens like themselves. Suppose individuation has not taken place before the teen years. In that case, a teen will try to show their individuality as a teenager and will likely have to learn from bad choices as they try and figure out what peer groups they belong to.

CHAPTER 11

PRAYING FOR OUR CHILDREN

A s parents, we can only do so much to mold and train our children. However, when we partner with our Heavenly Father, He can do more than we could possibly imagine. Our Heavenly Father is the master potter we can trust to mold our children into what He has designed them to be. Our children are His masterpieces. I know it's hard to believe, but He cares for them even more than we care for them.

As we train our children, we pray for wisdom and direction. We rely on God to show us the gifts in our children and how to love them best. We also need to pray for their development in each of the stages of their lives. We need to pray for their spiritual well-being and their understanding of spiritual things. We pray for their protection. We pray for God to guide their decisions that will determine their life course. As they get older, heading into the teen years, we pray more than ever before, and it doesn't stop there. As they move out of our homes and get married, we continue to pray for them and their families. 1 Thessalonians 5:17 NLT says, *"NEVER STOP PRAYING."* I know this applies to praying for our children.

Pray from Scripture

As we pray, it's important to remember that some of the most powerful prayers we can pray come from scripture. I am constantly learning how to take scripture and use it in my prayers and my confession over my kids. The Bible says that the scriptures are sharper than a two-edged sword. As scripture comes out of our mouths, it sets things in motion to bring protection, healing, and provision. Praying scripture has so much power because the scripture is what God already told us He would do.

It's essential to be specific in our prayers. We need to look at what our concerns are and what specific needs our children have. Instead of praying for God to be with our child, we can pray, "God, please keep my child safe from being bullied in school." Or, "Please keep my child safe from strangers and give my child discernment of people that might want to harm them."

I will share with you how I pray in different situations. In no way am I telling you how to pray because only the Holy Spirit can show you how to pray. But I'll give you some ideas of what I do. As you become more familiar with how to pray, you will start to recognize God leading you to pray specific prayers that will target your situation best.

Pray Before Your Baby is Born

The best time to begin praying for your child is before they are even born. It is never too early to start praying for your child. If your kids are older and you haven't started praying for them yet, you can start now. It is never too late.

In utero, the baby can hear your voice, and it is an excellent idea to pray out loud as you pray over your child. When I was pregnant, I prayed a lot about the health of my baby: healthy development for all organs and parts of their body, and a peaceful and safe delivery. I also prayed for their spiritual development even at this young age. The Bible talks about how

John the Baptist jumped in Elizabeth's womb as Mary spoke. Mary had come to see Elizabeth after the immaculate conception of Jesus. Babies can feel and respond to the Spirit of God even in the womb. I would also sing and worship often while I was pregnant. I prayed for my baby to feel God's presence.

Prayer for Unborn Baby

"Lord, thank you for blessing us with this child. I pray, Lord, that you would protect and watch over this baby as it develops inside me. Lord, I pray that you cause all of this child's organs to develop without any issues or deformities. I declare health over this child, in Jesus' name. I pray for divine, perfect health over the heart, kidneys, liver, adrenal glands, brain, lungs, digestive system, and stomach in Jesus' name. Lord, I pray that this child will sense your spirit even now. Lord, bathe this child in your peace and love as they are developing. I pray that they will grow to love you with all of their heart and desire you, Lord, more than anything in this world."

Pray for Help to Fill Their Needs

We have talked about emotional needs in childhood. Praying for guidance and help in filling your children's emotional needs is imperative. Your children's emotional needs are the foundation for everything. We will never be able to fill each of our children's needs perfectly, but with God's help, we can do better than if we relied on our own strength and understanding. Proverbs 3:5-7 Amp says, "5 Trust in and rely confidently on the Lord with all your heart And do not rely on your own insight or understanding. 6 In all your ways know and acknowledge and recognize Him. And He will make your paths straight, and smooth [removing obstacles that block your way]. 7 Do not be wise in your own eyes; Fear the Lord [with reverent awe and obedience] and turn [entirely] away from evil." As you rely on Him to show you areas of emotional lack, He will show you and help you resolve them.

Prayer for Help Recognizing Emotional Deficits

Heavenly Father,

I recognize my child has emotional needs. Lord, as I acknowledge you in my parenting, I need your help to recognize the emotional needs that are not being met in my child. Help me to recognize exactly what area my child needs more love. Lord, as I see the area that needs more love, give me wisdom to know how to fill it. Heavenly Father, help me stay diligent at tending the garden of my child's heart, watering each area with Your love flowing out of me to my child. Lord, bring experiences into our lives that will be evidence that Your love is flowing and multiplying.

In Jesus' Name,
Amen

God is There When We Can't Be

As our children grow and become more independent, we can't follow them around to ensure they are safe. Our children will go off to school and do other activities without us. It's hard to let go and let our children out of our site, especially during the times that we live in now. The world out there is so much more dangerous than ever before. What if they get hurt? What if they are bullied? What if they are making the wrong friends? What if a shooter breaks into the school? All these thoughts go through our minds when our kids aren't with us. We can't keep our children in a bubble and never let them leave. It comforts me to know that God is still there when we can't be. We can pray a prayer of protection over them. We can ask God to place a hedge or shield of protection around them to keep them safe from harm and to guard them against any tactics from the evil one. (2 Thessalonians 3:3; Psalm 33:20) We can ask God to help our children make the right decisions and have discernment when choosing their friends. We can also pray that they choose the right friends and that their friends will positively influence them.

As we pray for our kids, God will partner with us and help them live right. Therefore, we will not need to be disciplined as often. God can change the hearts of our children so that they want to do what's right. You can pray: "Lord, help my children to have clean hands and a pure heart and not tell lies." (Psalms 24:4-5)

There Comes a Time

To be perfectly transparent with you, I didn't realize the importance of praying for my children until my oldest child graduated and started heading down a road of rebellion. Up until this point, I believed that if I taught and disciplined my children correctly, that would be good enough. I thought that if I had control over my children as they grew up, they would naturally follow what I taught them. Well, I was so wrong.

As our firstborn graduated from high school, she started to veer away from what we taught her, and we no longer had any control over what she did. Eventually, our kids reach an age where we don't have to guide them as much as we once did. They start making their own decisions, and we hope that they will make decisions based on what we taught them growing up. We taught our daughter biblical principles and raised her with the knowledge of God, but to be honest, I didn't pray for her as I should have. During this time, as she was doing her own thing—opposite of what we taught her—I figured out that the only thing that I could do was pray.

For about a year and a half, she lived a life that was not glorifying God.

She was drinking, partying, and hanging out with the wrong crowd. It was a devastating time for us to see her going down this road. At this point, if we tried to give her any direction, she pushed us away and did the very opposite. She ended up moving out, and we wouldn't see her for a couple of weeks at a time. I learned very quickly that if there was anything I could do, it was to pray and pray hard. I prayed for her to turn back to God and for the new and harmful relationships to lose their appeal. I also prayed for her to remember how good it felt when she was walking with God. Finally, I prayed for the conviction of the Holy Spirit as she would do things that were against God's will.

It took some time, but little by little, we started to see a shift. My daughter began to come back around the house. She began to talk to me about little things again. Her friendships and associations started to shift. She began going to a Bible study with her new friends, and she started to recognize, once again, that life with God is the life she wanted. We moved out of state during this time, and she came with us. The move separated her from the friends she was hanging out with and gave her a fresh start. She started flourishing in her spiritual life once again. She is, to this day, serving God and married to a godly man. If I hadn't STOPPED trying to change her in my power and turned to God for help, she probably would still be living a life of struggles. God wants us to pray for our kids so that He can help us in raising them for His glory.

Preventative Prayer

I believe that when we pray for our kids, we can prevent behavioral issues before they get rooted. I think if I were praying for my firstborn before all the rebellion started, it could have been avoided or minimized. One of my sons has a problem with lying and being self-centered. When

I pray for this particular child, I pray specifically against those things. I ask God to get ahold of his heart and help him to desire to live a godly life. I also pray that my child feels conviction of the Holy Spirit when he is doing something wrong. I pray that my child will know what's right and wrong and for him to want to do what's right. Finally, I pray that all my children will want to please God and us in all that they do. When I pray for my son, I can see a difference in his behavior and attitude. I see God working in his heart to turn him from these unpleasant behaviors. When we pray, God does a more profound work in our kids than our discipline can do. Discipline is necessary, but praying for our kids is even more powerful.

My prayer for my son sounds like this, "Lord, I lift up _____ to you. I pray that you will get ahold of his heart and reveal to him who you are in his life. I pray that he will recognize your Holy Spirit and understand the ways of the Holy Spirit. I come against any lying and self-centered spirits functioning in him in Jesus' name. Lord, I speak honesty and self-lessness over him, in Jesus' name. Father God, help us and give us the wisdom to lead him into the fullness of his calling in You, and help us to train him up so he will glorify you in every area in his life. I pray, Lord, that you will keep him in the palm of your hands and lead him and guide him with your spirit. Help him decide to do what is right in your eyes and give him a desire to want to please you, Lord. In Jesus name, Amen." Also, when we discipline our children, we take time to reassure them and pray with them after discipline occurs. This is especially true if it's behaviors that they have been struggling with over and over again. As you pray with your child, you demonstrate how to seek God for the right behaviors and attitudes.

Guidance in Career Planning

Sometime in middle school, we start to pray more fervently for our children to have a direction of what God wants them to do for a career. It's crucial for our children to understand God's will for their life, especially when choosing a career. This timeframe is also necessary to know their identity and who God created them to be. When our kids are doing what God has called them to do, they will be happier and blessed in whatever they do. If our children know what God wants them to do before they graduate, it helps set the course for the next few years. Also, if our children are confident in their calling, they won't need to change majors in college or be confused about what direction to go.

When our children go into college, I pray for their safety and protection—physically, mentally, and spiritually. Physically, I pray for a hedge of protection over them to keep them from all harm. Mentally, I pray that God will give them His peace and that they will keep their thoughts on what is pure, right, honorable, excellent, and admirable (Philippians 4:8). Spiritually, I pray that they will be strong to withstand the influences that go against the knowledge of God and ask for God to give them the strength and ability to stand up for their beliefs. I pray for them to have the diligence to stay in the Word and to stay in prayer. I know this is what will keep them strong in their faith and give them the endurance to stand up against those things that try to tear them away from their faith. I also pray that God would remind them of His presence and that they would never forget how sweet it is to be in God's will. I pray for them to make friends that will encourage them in their faith and will be good influences in their lives. It's a brutal world out there, and they need all the prayers they can get to endure the pressures that this world places on their shoulders.

Praying For their Spouse

It is a good idea to pray for your child's future spouse even when your kids are little. As we pray for our kid's spouses, it helps ensure that they will have a better marriage, marry the right person, and continue to serve God when they get married. As I pray for my children's future spouse, I ask God to bless my child with a God-fearing, spirit-filled man or woman. I pray that my children would not take an interest in a man or woman that is not the one that God has selected for them. I pray that God would give them the wisdom to discern very quickly who is or who isn't their future spouse so that their hearts don't get wrapped up in the wrong person. Finally, I pray that my child will marry someone who truly seeks after God in everything they do and puts God first in their lives. I know that if they marry someone with these qualities, no matter what challenges marriage throws at them, they will endure it and prosper. As long as God is most important, everything else will fall into place. Modeling a healthy marriage to your kids is also important.

Beyond Marriage

After marriage, we still need to pray for our kids. Now, it's time to pray for the dynamics of their families as well. I continue to pray for their physical protection, and I also pray for their spiritual well-being. For my daughter, who just married, I pray that she and her husband continue to fervently seek God and not become lukewarm Christians. I pray for them both to pursue God separately and together. For my son-in-law, I pray that he would be the Priest of his household and that my daughter would be the godly mother and wife she is called to be. I pray that they will raise my grandchildren in a strong knowledge and presence of God and that they would be a household that chases after God with everything within them. Of course, there will be specific prayers that need to be prayed at different times of their lives, but this is just a general example of what I pray for regularly.

Powerful Declaration

This is a powerful declaration for your child and their spouse as a foundational prayer. I declare this daily.

Taken from Psalms 1:1-3: "Blessed [fortunate, prosperous, and favored by God] are all my children who do not walk in the counsel of the wicked [not following bad advice and examples], nor do they stand in the path of sinners, nor do they sit in the seat of scoffers. But my children and their spouses' delight is in the law of the Lord, And on Your law [Your precepts and teaching] my children [habitually] meditate day and night. And my children and their spouses will be like a tree firmly planted [and fed] by streams of water, Which yields its fruit in its season; Its leaf does not wither; And in whatever they do, my children prosper [and comes to maturity]." Amen

Wrapping it Up

As I wrap up this chapter, I want to give you some scriptures that are guidelines to help you pray for your children. I will provide you with the chapter and verse reference so that you can study these verses in your personal devotional time. Still, I will put them in personalized wording so that you can see how I would use them to pray for my children. Writing the entire scripture out on an index card will help you keep relevant scripture in front of you. This will help you target your prayers until you see a breakthrough.

Praying For Your Child's Salvation, Romans 10:9

Lord, I pray that _____ will confess with his/her mouth that Jesus Christ is Lord (recognizing His power, authority, and majesty as God), and _____ will believe in his/her heart that God raised Him from the dead and _____ will be saved.

Being Lead By the Spirit, Galatians 5:25

I pray, Lord, that_____ will be lead by the Spirit.

Following God's Ways, Psalms 119:32

Lord, help _____ to run the way of Your commandments with purpose and give _____ a heart that is willing.

Healthy Fear of God, Jeremiah 32:3

Lord, Give _____ one heart and one purpose: that they may reverently fear God forever, for their own good and for the good of all their children after them.

Being Strong in Their Faith, Colossians 2:6-7

I declare that _____ will walk in union with the Lord, reflecting His character in the things he/she does and says. I also declare that _____ will be deeply rooted in Christ and continually built up in Him-becoming increasingly more established in his/her faith.

Knowing Their Acceptance in Him, Jeremiah 1:5

I declare that _____ will know that before _____ was formed in the womb You knew and approved of him/her as Your chosen instrument and was consecrated to God as His own.

Knowing They Have Purpose, Ephesians 2:10

Lord, I declare that _____ knows that he/she is Your workmanship, (Your own master work, a work of art), created in You for good works, which You prepared beforehand and _____ is taking paths which You already set and that _____ would walk in them.

Honesty and Integrity, Psalms 25:21

I pray, Lord, that my children will have honesty and integrity and it will protect them.

Having Right Motives, Philippians 2:3-5

Father God, help my children do nothing from selfishness or empty conceit, but with an attitude of humility, regarding others as more important than themselves. Help them not merely look out for their own personal interests, but also for the interests of others.

Fruits of the Spirit, Galatians 5:22

Father God, I pray that my children will have these fruits in their lives: love, joy, peace, patience, kindness, goodness, faithfulness, gentleness, and self-control.

Love for God's Word, Psalms 19:10

God, help my children find your words more desirable than gold that is sweeter than honey.

Respect, 1 Peter 2:17

Lord, help my children to show proper respect to everyone as your words says.

Purity, Psalm 51:10

Father, please create in my children a clean heart and renew a right spirit within them.

Perseverance, Hebrews 12:1

Heavenly father, help my children to run with endurance the race that you set before them.

Compassion, Colossians 3:12

Lord, I pray that my children will be clothed with tenderhearted mercy, kindness, humility, gentleness, and patience.

Faith, Luke 17:6

Father God, I pray that my children have faith that moves mountains.

Boldness, 2 Timothy 1:7

I declare that, Lord, You did not give _____ a spirit of timidity or cowardice or fear, but You gave _____ a spirit of power and of Love and of sound judgment and personal discipline.

Good Work Ethic and a Servant's Heart, Ephesians 6:7

Lord, help my children to work and serve with enthusiasm and to please you and not man.

Passion for God, Psalm 63:8

God, help my children to cling to you as your hand upholds them.

Being a Witness, Matthew 5:16

Lord, let my children's light shine before men so that you will be glorified.

Sound Mind, 2 Timothy 1:7

Father God, thank you that my children do not have a spirit of fear but of power, love, and sound minds.

Good Meditation, Philippians 4:8

Heavenly Father, help my children think and meditate on things that are pure, good, and praiseworthy.

Choosing Right Friends, 1 Corinthians 15:33

Lord, help my children choose right friends so that their ways will not be corrupted.

Wayward Teen, Acts 26:18

Lord, open _____ spiritual eyes so that he/she will turn from darkness to light and from the power of Satan to the power of God. I declare that _____ will receive forgiveness and release from his/her sins and will receive the inheritance of the sanctified.

CHAPTER 12

IT'S A JOURNEY,
NOT A FINAL DESTINATION

I remember going through prayer lines, taking classes, and reading books, thinking that I would instantly be a better parent on the other side. The truth is, I had to walk it out, one step at a time. Emotional healing on the road to better parenting is a daily walking out of submitting to the things God shows us to do. It is allowing God to turn our depleted and hardened heart into hearts of flesh. As we are able to respond better than we had before, rising above offenses and triggers, we will become safer and connect emotionally with our children. In order to see our fruit change, from rotten to good fruit, we must allow God's word to transform us and renew our minds. The more time we spend with Jesus, allowing Him to remove the toxic or hardened areas of our hearts, the better parents we become.

As you go through changes, you will have good days and bad days, successes and failures, breakthroughs and roadblocks. As long as you keep pressing forward toward your goals of healing, you will succeed in becoming a better version of yourself each day.

Filter Through Emotional Needs

One significant key that I have learned is to use emotional needs to evaluate your heart and your fruit on a daily basis. From there, as you parent your children, it is also important to filter your responses through those same emotional needs of your children. Mark and I remind each other regularly, as we respond or react to our children, to first filter it through nurturing responses, unconditional love, affirmation, approval, or encouragement.

Here's one example: Elisha, our oldest son, was starting to date. We wanted to keep him accountable, so we asked him to share his location with us as he left the house. Eli expressed that this bothered him. We couldn't figure out why it would bother him if he wasn't doing anything wrong. One day, he expressed very passionately his frustration with us requesting this of him. He said, "I feel like this is an invasion of my privacy." When he said that, I instantly knew that we were causing a deficit to occur in the area of RESPECT. We were not respecting his privacy and he felt it. I learned that any relational problems we have with our children can be avoided and/or traced back to these emotional needs. When you speak to your children, be careful to filter your words through affirmation. When you notice a behavior you don't like, filter your response through unconditional love to make sure they know you love them no matter what. This simple tool will help you quickly evaluate how to respond to your child in each situation that arises.

It's Never Too Late

If you have older children, it is never too late to bring healing to their hearts and to that child's relationship. As I gained healing, I realized how much we could've done better and how differently we should've parented, had we known better. We currently have five adult children. As we learned about the deficit of emotional needs in our parenting, I thought it was too late to reverse the damage that had been done. But, as our hearts healed, our responses dramatically changed, and our children noticed the difference.

Healing occurs as your responses towards them shift and change. You can start to bring healing by allowing them to talk about the things that hurt them in the past without getting defensive or upset with them. Suppose you recognize areas where you failed to meet your child's emotional needs or hurt them somehow. In that case, you can open the conversation and talk about it with them. In either case, the response should focus on apologizing and owning whatever you did to cause pain. When apologizing, you mustn't use any excuses or reasoning in your conversation because it will negate the apology. If there is any language that sounds like reasoning, it can come across as insincere. As you apologize and talk about the situation with them, it should allow a release of the pain in their heart and cause reconciliation.

Instances of control strained the relationship between my daughter and me. I didn't recognize my behavior as controlling back then. I thought I was protecting her and being a good parent. But, as I tried to control her and her decisions, she became very resentful, put up walls, and grew distant.

When my daughter was about 17 years old, she began dating. We disapproved of the relationships she was choosing. We feared that she would choose a young man that would create an unhealthy relationship and possibly marriage. I feared that we would lose her if she married the wrong man. We tried to control the situation by telling her she couldn't see them. Later on, when we couldn't influence her decisions, we would persistently and dominantly make our opinions known. My daughter felt very controlled, and it dramatically affected our relationship for years to come. Before I gained healing, we talked about our relationship and what happened back then. I tried to rationalize my behavior and explain why I did what I did. Still, it didn't bring us any closer or create a resolution. It just made things worse. After I gained healing, I apologized for trying to control her and for not trusting her decisions and choices. At that stage in her life, she needed me to encourage and support her while trying to make right choices instead of controlling her and making decisions for her. I asked her to forgive me, and we began rebuilding our relationship.

Knowing the Truth

I'm sure you've heard the scripture, John 8:32: And you will know the truth and truth will set you free. Knowing the truth will set you free, but it's not enough to just know it in your head. You must know it in your heart. In order for the truth of God's word to become your reality, you need to meditate on it day and night. Meditating on scripture doesn't have to take large amounts of time, but you need to be consistent in order for it to change what you've believed for so long. Just like I mentioned in the last chapter, you need to write scripture, your nuggets of truth, on an index card, memorize them, meditate on them, declare them, and pray God makes them your new reality. Every time you are faced with the lie of your past, push it aside and embrace the truth. You are good enough! God has equipped you to be the parent you need to be to your children. You are not a failure! You can do ALL things through Christ. Your past does not have to dictate your future. Just because your family has been dysfunctional for generations doesn't mean you have to continue the pattern. It can stop with you. Search the scriptures and find your story and your truth.

Never Give Up

What are you going to do on those days that you blow it? Take a deep breath and give yourself permission to start the day over. There are going to be days that you struggle more than others. You can use those challenging moments to grow in your healing as you process your responses through the healing principles. Remember to gain P.O.W.E.R. over your past. Decide not to stay stuck in those old behaviors and use those challenging moments to grow. Your challenges can take you to a new level of growth.

In those moments when you are struggling, what do you do? Admit you aren't responding as you should and ask God to help you. Each time you make a decision in those moments to adjust your thoughts and actions to line up with God's word, it's an opportunity to "pass a test"; to go to a higher level in parenting. If you choose to lean on God and allow Him to help you, you will grow in that moment.

When your responses are harsh, what should we NOT do? Don't feed off of bad choices and continue to spiral out of control. Don't come into agreement with the lies of the enemy, thinking you are a failure. Rise above the lies and believe the truth. Do not forget God loves you unconditionally and He is here to help you be better.

James 1:4 says, *"And let endurance have its perfect result and do a thorough work, so that you may be perfect and completely developed [in your faith], lacking in nothing."*

Expect to be Tested

Each time we gain a new level of healing, we are going to have a new level of testing. You see, the enemy doesn't want us to be free from the bondage of bad attitudes and wrong behaviors. He is going to try to cause us to think about things that will ignite old behaviors and try to get us to go back to the way we used to be.

Be patient with yourself and keep working those principles of healing. We will always be growing and gaining healing every day. Be consistent and intentional. When you have a bad day, you need to refocus your attention on God. Remember what He has taught you in His Word and throughout this process in your healing. Remind yourself of what you were like before you started on this path of healing in your life. We need to remember that we are going through a process of healing and we will continue to be in this process. God peels us back like an onion, one layer at a time. He heals us of our pains and hurts, one layer at a time.

In this process of being changed into the likeness of Christ, if you keep pressing forward, you will not fail. When you have moments of setback, you need to get back up and stay in the fight. Focus on the destination, but realize it is a lifelong journey.

After reading this book you may be thinking,
"Now what?"

I'm glad you asked!

We want to walk with you on this parenting journey.
We have resources available that will help you connect emotionally to your children so that you can lead them effectively with love, confidence, and grace.

**Please visit us at
BeyondYourUpbringing.com
to learn more.**

ABOUT THE AUTHOR

Denise Engelbrecht has a passion for family and a mission to help parents break free from past hurts that keep them stuck in unsuccessful cycles. Her message comes from her fascinating journey—she beat the odds, broke patterns of abuse, and established life patterns of renewal. Having raised seven children, she has had plenty of experience practicing what she teaches. She enjoys strengthening others in their faith and in their Christ-centered families by teaching biblical principles. Her goal is to encourage people to overcome the challenges of their past through her books and her speaking. Denise attended Roberts Wesleyan College for Communications where she met her husband, Mark. Denise enjoys working with Living Waters Ministry, teaching, transformational public speaking, ministering emotional healing, and personal coaching.

JOIN US FOR A **HEALING THE HEART** RETREAT

- **A Healing the Heart retreat is truly a life-changing experience.**

- **Healing the Heat breaks you free from the pain of the past.**

- **When your heart is healed you will respond instead of react.**

- **Responding from a healed heart gives you the ability to heal your family.**

- **Healing the heart repositions you to experience life in a new way.**

- **Pastors Lee and Denise Boggs have led thousands of people just like you to a life of wholeness.**

SCHEDULE YOUR RETREAT TODAY AT
LIVINGWATERSMINISTRY.COM

CPSIA information can be obtained
at www.ICGtesting.com
Printed in the USA
JSHW042146270222
23245JS00001B/6